ARIZONA'S BACK ROADS

a Travel Guide to Ghosts, Outlaws, and Miners

Julie Ferguson

Schiffer Publishing Ltd

4880 Lower Valley Road • Atglen, PA 19310

Designed by Molly Shields
Type set in !Sketchy Times/Book Antiqua

ISBN: 978-0-7643-4607-1
Printed in China

Schiffer Books are available at special discounts for bulk purchases for sales promotions or premiums. Special editions, including personalized covers, corporate imprints, and excerpts can be created in large quantities for special needs. For more information contact the publisher:

Published by Schiffer Publishing, Ltd.
4880 Lower Valley Road
Atglen, PA 19310
Phone: (610) 593-1777; Fax: (610) 593-2002
E-mail: Info@schifferbooks.com

For the largest selection of fine reference books on this and related subjects, please visit our website at
www.schifferbooks.com.
We are always looking for people to write books on new and related subjects. If you have an idea for a book, please contact us at
proposals@schifferbooks.com.

This book may be purchased from the publisher.
Please try your bookstore first.
You may write for a free catalog.

All images by the author unless otherwise noted.

Epigraph

Treat the earth well. It was not given to you by your parents; it was loaned to you by your children.

We do not inherit the Earth from our Ancestors; we borrow it from our children.

–*Ancient Indian Proverb*

Dedication

*For my husband and his amazing support; for
my children who believed in their mother; and for
Sharon Day, my co-author on other books, trip
buddy, and best friend who helped take my dreams
and make them a reality.*

Acknowledgments

I would like to thank my husband for his belief in me and helping me to see my potential. His patience let me take the many road trips to achieve my goals, improve my photography, and visit the many places I have shared in this book.

Also, I would like to thank my friend and co-author (of other projects), Sharon Day. I would still be lost and wondering what to do with my life if you hadn't pulled me up, showing me that I can utilize my natural talents, and not to be afraid to go for it.

Plus, I would like to acknowledge all the small mining towns, Wild West cemeteries, and Indian ruins around Arizona. Thanks for your hospitality. You made visiting your places a pleasure while we took pictures of your many abandoned structures.

Finally, I would like to thank the Bird Cage Theatre in Tombstone for being the best host while we roamed your place in the dark for three hours looking for ghosts.

Contents

Map Key

1A – Besh-Ba-Gowah
1B – Devil's Chasm & Pueblo Canyon Ruins
1C – Cold Spring Canyon Ruins & Copper
       Forks Canyon Ruins
1D – Montezuma Castle
1E – Walnut Canyon National Monument
1F – Navajo National Monument
1G – Canyon de Chelly National Monument
1H – Tuzigoot National Monument
1I – Palatki Heritage Site
1J – Casa Grande Ruins National Monument
1K – Mesa Grande
1L – Fortaleza
1M – Gatlin
1N – Sedona
1O – Painted Rock Petroglyph Site
1P – The V-Bar-V Heritage Site
1Q – Rock Art Ranch
1R – White Tanks Mountain Regional Preserve
1S – South Mountain Park
2A – Vulture Mine
2B – Globe
2C – Bisbee
2D – Jerome
2E – Tombstone
2F – Fairbank
3A – Prescott
3B – Phoenix
3C – Benson
3D – Tucson
3E – Yuma Territorial Prison
3F – Superior
4A – Discarded Motel (Gila Bend)
4B – Bee Apartments (Miami)
4C – The Relinquish Trailer Park (Mobile)
4D – The Sugar Beet Factory (Glendale)
4E – The Domes (Casa Grande)
4F – Hayden Flour Mill (Tempe)
5A – Adamsville Cemetery
5B – Old Congress Cemetery
5C – Fairbank Cemetery
5D – Goodyear-Ocotillo Cemetery
5E – Morristown Cemetery
5F – Mayer Cemetery
6A – The Thing?
6B – The Grand Canyon
6C – White Mountains

6D – Mogollon Rim
6E – Tovrea Castle
6F – Mystery Castle
6G – The Superstition Mountains
6H – Bird Cage Theatre Museum
6I – Phoenix Zoo
6J – Wildlife World Zoo & Aquarium
6K – Anthem (Ghost Hitchhiker)
6L – U.S. Highway 93 (Ghost Bus)
6M – Highway 666

For best results, check websites
and other visitor information
before visiting, in case the
information listed here has changed.

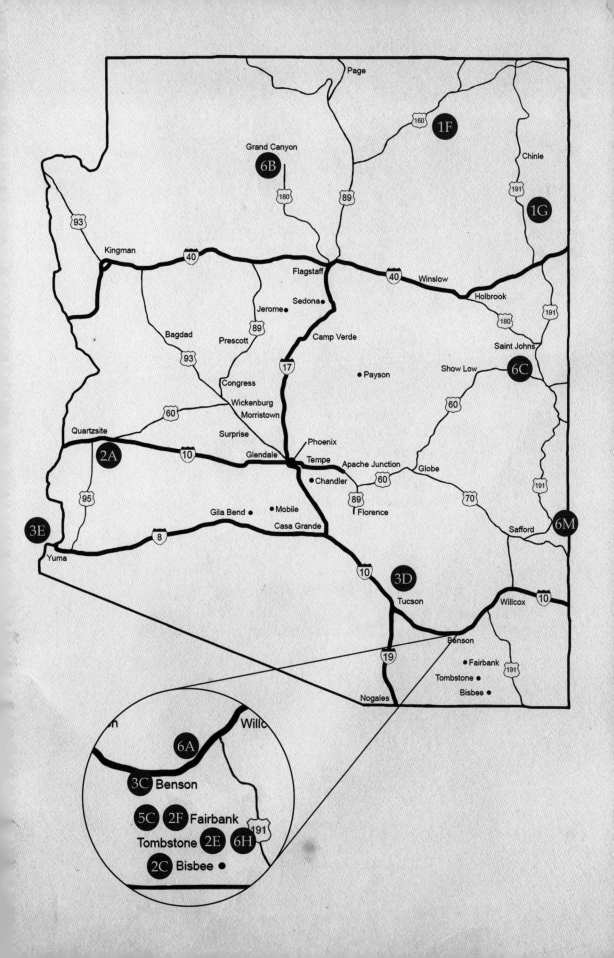

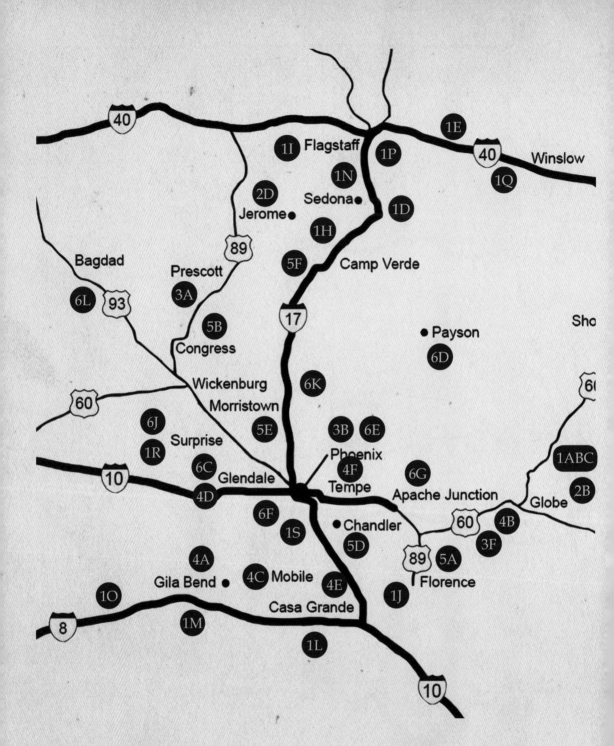

Introduction

This book is a tour guide through some of the remarkable past and perplexing conundrums that make up the state of Arizona and the Southwest desert.

Visit the Native American ruins where the tattered decomposing walls of their dwellings are all that is left, along with pottery shards, handmade tools, and astonishing petroglyphs etched on boulders revealing the stories of what life was like many centuries ago.

Tour of the mysterious city of Sedona with its breathtaking scenery, unexplained healing powers, baffling vortexes, and sightings of UFOs. You will have plenty of information about this amazing city to make your trip to here enjoyable and rewarding.

Discover six Southwestern mining towns and the history of their establishments. What would bring people to the Southwest with the dangers of Indian attacks, extreme heat, and a wasteland of little water? It was the minerals found in the soil and the hope of a better life that drove the families, businessmen, and greedy individuals to a life in the desert. The mining towns prospered in their heyday and enjoyed a booming population. When the mines dried up, most of the people moved away. Today, these settlements are either abandoned, considered ghost towns, or surviving by the tourists and handful of residents who call these places home.

Arizona has many mining towns where the law was kept by marshals and sheriffs. There were many outlaws who laid their hats in some of these Wild West towns while raising havoc. I centered on some I thought had the more interesting stories to be told. They left their mark in history as thugs, thieves, and murderers. Life was not easy for these sinful men and women and they survived by any means possible.

A number of these outlaws were buried somewhere in the Southwest desert. The old west cemeteries were once well maintained and thriving with beautiful carved headstones. Many decades later, these cemeteries can be found neglected, forgotten with broken headstones and rusty fences. The shrubbery is overgrown and hiding many of the grave sites entirely.

Along with the cemeteries, there are many places around Arizona and the Southwest that are now abandoned and falling apart. What many might see as atrophy, others see a beauty that has been left behind. The history and stories of these places are just as interesting as the decaying walls and missing ceilings of the structures that fell between the cracks of time.

The Southwest is vast and so are the varied mysteries found in the barren lands. Urban legends have been told for many decades about the ghosts wandering the desert, along with fascinating mummies and fossils buried in the dirt. The mountains hold many mesmerizing stories of lost treasures and castles made of reclaimed items.

Join me for a tour of all these places with stories of their pasts, and what you will find if you visit them today. I have mapped out the locations of the ruins, mining towns, abandoned places, and the streets where outlaws once walked to help you plan your Arizona trip with ease. The key for the map will give you the chapter number where you can read about the location, a letter code, and the location name.

Enjoy the amenities that the Southwest and Arizona have to offer, while seeing it all from your car.

CHAPTER 1

House of the Spirits

Besh-Ba-Gowah Archaeological Park, Globe, 2010.

For thousands of years, tucked in the mountains or scattered amongst the desolate dirt floors of the Southwest desert, Indian ruins of ancient civilizations can be found. These past inhabitants left their partially ruined structures, pottery shards, painted rocks, and tools, leaving us to speculate how they were able to survive the harsh desert. The Sinagua, Salado, and Hohokam people were some of the Native Americans who once thrived around the 12th century and then mysteriously disappeared in the vast desert wasteland. Amid the ruins are places where petroglyphs can be found. These boulders have various symbols etched on them, giving us a glimpse of life in the ancient Native American era. Also found in Arizona is a tranquil and spiritual city where the rocks are as red as the sunset and unexplained events have been known to exist.

LONG FORGOTTEN SALADO RUINS

The Salado people existed around the 15th century and lived in the Tonto Basin region located in the southeastern part of Arizona. What make the Salado different were their abilities to create unique pottery, the adobe built structures in each village, and burying their dead instead of incinerating them like other cultures. They farmed their crops using canals they constructed to water the fields. They grew food for eating and cotton for making cloth. They also hunted the local game for food. The entire Salado clan existed for over 200 years and then mysteriously disappeared.

THE BESH-BA-GOWAH ARCHAEOLOGICAL PARK

Besh-Ba-Gowah sign, Globe, 2010.

Besh-Ba-Gowah two-story ruins, Globe, 2011.

The Besh-Ba-Gowah Archaeological Park is located on the outskirts of Globe, Arizona, and only a mile and a quarter from its historic downtown. It is an old pueblo ruin and is approximately 700 years old. This remarkable site's skeletal remains are well preserved for all who visit and want to take a walk back in time.

The history of this place takes us as far back as the 13th century when many Native American dwellings were built in this area along the Pinal Creek. The region was ideal for these settlements to thrive with the abundance of water, the large assortment of desert foliage, and the perfect weather for growing crops almost year round.

The structure of this community was built as a defense mechanism against enemies or other dangers to those who lived there. The entrance was through a narrow corridor with no openings to view the outside. The passage takes you between the dwellings to the central plaza, where ceremonies were held and many of the dead were buried. The walls were constructed of sand, clay, large stones, and are several inches thick. Each building was two or more stories high, using the ground level for storage while the families lived in the upper levels. It was believed the Salado Indians were a highly developed group of people with remarkable abilities to create utensils, decorative pottery, and colorful cotton cloths. The many extraordinary desert plants that surround the structures were used by this pre-Columbian tribe for food, construction materials, and dyes.

The Salado inhabitants remained in the Besh-Ba-Gowah for over 200 years until they simply just vanished. Some speculated that the change in weather conditions had depleted the water supply, which contributed to their

The entrance and narrow passage to the ruins, Globe, 2011.

From the second floor of the building is a view of the central plaza, dwelling ruins, and visitor center, Globe, 2011.

demise. The dwellings stood abandoned for more than 200 years until the Apache people made it their home.

The name Besh-Ba-Gowah was bestowed upon the community by the Apache people and signifies "place of metal" or "metal camp."

Today, many of the buildings and walls are still standing. The passage remains and takes you between the skeletal leftovers of the dwellings to the central plaza. Some of the structures have been restored to their original status for visitors to get an idea of the living conditions of the Salado people. The wood ladders have been re-created for visitors to climb to the second floor where many of the pottery pieces found in the excavation are now displayed. When the area was dug up, ladders, pottery, utensils, jewelry, and other furbishing items were found in remarkable shape. From the second floor there is another ladder leading to the roof of the pueblo. The roof was used as another way to walk from one structure to another.

Also located on the site is an Ethnobotanical garden with an amazing variety of desert plant life, and the Besh-Ba-Gowah Museum, which displays artifacts of the Salado, a model of the ruins as it probably appeared in the 13th century, and a wonderful variety of gifts.

DEVIL'S CHASM AND PUEBLO CANYON RUINS

Devil's Chasm and Pueblo Canyon Ruins are located in the Sierra Ancha Wilderness near Cherry Creek in the Tonto National Forest. To get to the location of the ruins, you must be prepared for a sheer climb on a narrow path. The trek to Devil's Chasm is approximately a four-hour round-trip hike. The passage to Pueblo Canyon Ruins is a six-mile voyage that takes almost five hours round-trip. These Salado ruins are carefully maintained and in amazing condition. If you visit these remains, they ask that you please respect their delicate nature by leaving things the way you found them.

VISITOR INFORMATION

Directions to Devil's Chasm and Pueblo Canyon Ruins: to get to both sites from Phoenix, head east on Highway 60 towards Globe. Right before entering Globe, turn left onto Highway 188 (also known as 88) and travel around 14.4 mile to the Highway 288 exit. Make a right turn on 288, drive over a bridge, and travel 6.7 miles to Cherry Creek Road (or Forest Road 203). Turn right on the dirt road and drive 8.8 miles to Coon Creek FR #203 to a fork in the road. Veer to the right, cross a creek, drive another 13.3 miles, pass the Ellison Ranch, where the road gets more rugged, until you get to a Forest Service sign that reads:

"Sierra Ancha Cliff Dwellings: Prehistoric cliff dwellings are located in several of the rugged canyons within and near the Sierra Ancha Wilderness. They were built between 1280 and 1350 AD by Indians known presently as the 'Salado'. Why they chose to utilize this challenging environmental zone is not yet fully understood. Cliff dwellings are fragile and irreplaceable. Please do not climb on the walls or roofs or cause any other form of injury or disturbance. Violators are subject to arrest, fines and or imprisonment."

There are plenty of places to park and an area to set up camp, if you want to rest the night before you set out on your trip to Devil's Chasm and Pueblo Canyon Ruins or any of the other Salado dwellings located in the Sierra Ancha Wilderness.

* They do suggest you drive a high-profile vehicle because the road is a bit rough and rocky.

ADDITIONAL RUINS

A couple more ruins located in the Sierra Ancha Wilderness are the Cold Spring Canyon Ruins and Copper Forks Canyon Ruins. The Sierra Ancha, which means "Wide Mountain," not only has an abundant amount of forests, but many Salado cliff dwellings are tucked in its rock mountains. Many of these ancient living quarters were discovered by Dr. Emil W. Haury and the Gila Pueblo Project in 1930. Since 1981 until today, Dr. Richard C. Lange is keeping the project alive.

VISITOR INFORMATION

Tonto National Forest
Website: www.fs.usda.gov/tonto

Sierra Ancha Wilderness
Websites: www.wilderness.net and www.fs.fed.us

Gila Pueblo Project
Website: www.statemuseum. arizona.edu/research/final_sierra_ ancha_rpt.shtml

ANCIENT CLIFF DWELLINGS

Throughout the state of Arizona, there are several ancient Native American ruins built in the cliffs of the Rocky Mountains. They were constructed in the 12th century and made of limestone, mud, or other various materials found in the region. The cliffs offered protection from all the dangers surrounding the settlement. Many of the dwellings are remarkably well preserved and worth a visit.

MONTEZUMA CASTLE

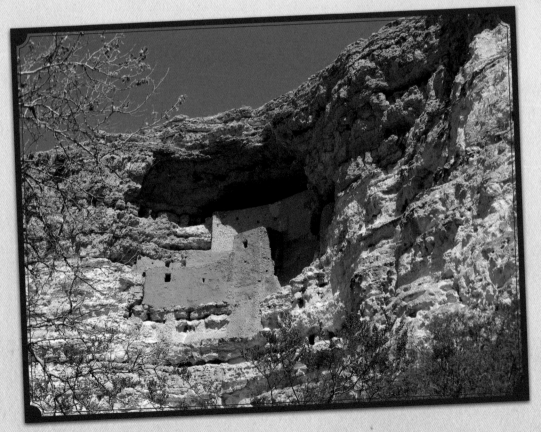

Montezuma Castle, near Sedona, 2011.

Castle A, Montezuma Castle, near Sedona, 2011.

Montezuma Castle is tucked in the mountains and located just outside Sedona in the Verde Valley. The cliff dwelling got its name because the building's foundation resembled an Aztec lodging. The extraordinary structure was built by the southern Sinagua people in the 12th century. Sinagua is Spanish for "without water." They used limestone, which is a soft material causing varying breakage over a long period of time, to build their abodes. Because Montezuma Castle is wedged tightly inside the rock cliffs, it has been protected by the elements and has remained intact for over 600 years. For that reason, this historic monument is one of the most successfully preserved early ruins in the Southwest.

The five-story dwelling, with its twenty rooms, is about 100 feet above Beaver Creek, which was used as their water source. It was speculated that they built the structure high in the mountains because the spot offered protection from the desert elements and their enemies. Below the cliff lodgings and along the base of the rock face, sits Castle A. This structure was also constructed of limestone and is almost completely gone from being worn down by time and the difficult Arizona weather.

The Sinagua people were hunters, gatherers, and artisans. The area had an abundant supply of deer, antelope, rabbit, bear, muskrat, and duck. They gathered many of the local plants, vegetables, and cotton they grew using their skillfully constructed canals for irrigation. They made their own stone tools, fashioned rocks for grinding corn, wove clothes from cotton, and used the red rock materials for their pottery. The red rocks were abundant in the surrounding area.

Beaver Creek near Montezuma Castle, 2011.

The Montezuma Castle Sinagua people lived in the high-rise rock apartments for over 400 years before vanishing mysteriously. By the early 1400s, the cliff and Castle A homes were vacated and left abandoned by the Sinagua. One speculation for their unknown disappearance could be too many citizens living in the cramped settlement and not enough space to move around or sleep. Some believe it was the severe weather changes causing the water to dry up, which harmed their food supply. Without the water, the animals would leave; in addition the surrounding plants and all their crops would die. Another theory is that a plague, diseases, or too many fights ending in death may have caused the Sinagua people's extinction. Whatever the reason, they left us an outstanding place to view and wonder about.

When the Montezuma Castle's tours first began sometime in the 1930s, people were able to get a close-up look at the structure tucked in the cliff. Visitors walked along a dirt path and climbed a succession of ladders up the side of the steep mountain. When arriving at the dwelling, they were able to step inside the tiny rooms the Sinagua once lived in. In 1951, because of the deteriorating limestone walls, tours no longer consisted of admittance to the ruins. Now we have to admire it from afar.

Today, sightseers walk through the visitor center to gain access to the site. Inside the visitor center, there is a museum, book store, and gift shop. After paying the fee, people walk out a set of doors to a line of pottery once used by the Sinagua people. A short distance to the right, up high and wedged into the mountainside, the incredible ruins can be observed.

It is amazing how well preserved the structure appears. A short distance on the path is the site for Castle A—not much left standing of the edifice, just partial walls. It is hard to imagine the structure as once being five stories high.

Around the corner is Beaver Creek; the picnic area is located amongst the many trees.

The last item on the path is a model of Montezuma Castle without the front walls. This tiny recreation gives visitors an idea of what it was like to live in the high-rise rock apartments.

Despite the fact they were constructed in the 13th to early 15th centuries, the cliff dwellings are in remarkable condition. The people who occupied the lower and upper rock habitats were farmers and hunters who feasted off the local animals and vegetation. They created colorful pottery and wove complex patterns on fabric, which can be found in many places around the Southwest. Those interested will also be treated with a Visitor Center museum on the premises with many of their items on display, models of the dwellings, and a history of the people who once called this place home.

VISITOR INFORMATION

Website: www.nps.gov/moca

Address: P.O. Box 219, Camp Verde, AZ 86322

Phone: (928) 567-3322

Hours: open daily from 8 a.m. to 5 p.m.; seven days a week (except Christmas Day).

Fees: adults (16 and older) $5; children (under 16) free

Directions: follow I-17 to exit 289 (located 90 minutes north of Phoenix and 45 minutes south of Flagstaff).

* Dogs are allowed in the park, but need to be on a leash no longer than six feet.

TONTO NATIONAL MONUMENT

Despite the fact that the Tonto National Monument was constructed in the 13th to early 15th centuries, the cliff dwellings are in remarkable condition. The people who occupied the Lower and Upper rock habitats were farmers and hunters who feasted off the local animals and vegetation. They created colorful pottery and wove complex patterns on fabric, which can be found around many places around the Southwest. You will also be treated with a Visitor Center museum on the premises with many of their items on display, models of the dwellings, and a history of the people who once called this place home.

VISITOR INFORMATION

Website: www.nps.gov/tont/index.htm

Hours: daily, 8 a.m. to 5 p.m. (except Christmas Day)

Fees: adults (16 and older) $3; children (under 16) free

Directions: there are a couple of ways to find this monument from the city of Phoenix. Take State Highway 60 (Superstition Freeway) east to Globe/Miami. From there turn left and travel northwest on State Highway 188. It is approximately 25 miles from the turnoff till you arrive at Tonto National Monument.

The other route is a bit rougher on vehicles, but will get you there much quicker. From Phoenix, take State Highway 88 (Apache Trail) and travel 47 miles to your destination. Half of the highway is asphalt, but the other half is gravel. If you are planning to take the Upper Cliff Dwelling tour, this route is not an option.

* Lower Cliff Dwelling trail closes to uphill travel at 4 p.m.

WALNUT CANYON NATIONAL MONUMENT

Rock Cliffs near Flagstaff, 2011.

The rock apartments located in the cliffs 7.5 miles east of Flagstaff were built as far back as the 1100s. Like many of the other Native American ancient sites, the Sinagua people originally lived in these dwellings. In typical Sinagua fashion, they mysteriously disappeared sometime in the middle 1200s and left their homes abandoned. The monument has been maintained by the U.S. National Park Service and has a couple of trails that go to the ruins. The Island Trail is a one-mile, paved trail to several dwellings where visitors can walk through the tiny rooms. This trek will take an hour to accomplish. The Rim Trail takes half the time and presents breathtaking views of the canyon and an area to sit near the rim to enjoy the scenery.

The ruins are only part of what can be seen when you visit the park. Walnut Canyon National Monument has a picnic section and a Visitor Center with a bookstore displaying all kinds of artifacts that were found during excavation of the ruins.

VISITOR INFORMATION

Website: www.nps.gov/waca/index.htm

Hours: 9 a.m. to 5 p.m. (November to April); 8 a.m. to 5 p.m. (May to October)

Fees: adults (16 and older) $5; children (under 16) free

Directions: The location is around 7.5 miles east of Flagstaff. From Flagstaff, travel east on Interstate 40, take the 204 exit, and then head south. Another 3 miles to the Walnut Canyon Visitor Center.

* Open: all year (except Christmas Day), with extended hours from May to October.

Tours are given all year long by Rangers, who discuss the history of the ruins, and field trips are offered for groups of school children.

NAVAJO NATIONAL MONUMENT

This Anasazi cliff dwelling has two sizeable rock living spaces known as Betatakin and Keet Seel. Maintained by the U.S. National Park Service, visitors will find three self-guided rim trails (Sandal, Aspen, and Canyon View) that offer splendid views of the entire area. The Betatakin guided tour is a five-mile trek. On this three- to five-hour round-trip excursion, discover the 135-room rock face apartments wedged deep in the cliffs. The Keet Seel jaunt provides the trail to the 160-room dwelling and is a four- to six-hour hour trek each way. Anyone interested in taking this tour must make reservations ahead of time, limiting groups to twenty people, and have a permit to be in the area, which can be purchased at the Visitor Center. This tour is also limited to the months of May through early September.

VISITOR INFORMATION

Website: www.nps.gov/nava/index.htm

Phone: (928) 672-2700

Hours: 8 a.m. to 5:30 p.m. (May to September) summer; 9 a.m. to 5 p.m. (September to May the following year) winter; everyday

Fees: Call for information on guided tours. Free for all three of the self-guided trails on mesa top. The campgrounds are free.

The Navajo National Monument is open all year long and has longer hours in the summertime. Both Sunset View and Canyon View campgrounds are open all summer. Sunset View is also open in the winter and has water.

Directions: the location is at the end of State Highway 564 off of US Highway 160.

CANYON DE CHELLY NATIONAL MONUMENT

Canyon De Chelly National Monument, 2009.

Just about 210 miles northeast of Flagstaff sits another Anasazi cliff dwelling ruin. These were also constructed from the 1100s and the 1300s. Deep inside the Navajo Nation, these sacred lands are maintained by the inhabitants. The Navajo people are willing to allow guests to walk their lands, but not all places are accessible to the populace. Those who want to take a self-guided tour of the area have three choices: There are two paved picturesque roads to the south and north rims, and those provide a magnificent view of the canyon. The other trek is 2.5 miles on the White House Ruins Trail and slopes down 600 feet to the bottom of the canyon. If there is an interest in seeing more of the canyon, a permit will be needed, as well as an official guide.

VISITOR INFORMATION

Website: www.nps.gov/cach/index.htm

Hours: open daily all year; 8 a.m. to 5 p.m. (Closed Christmas Day.)

Fees: no entrance fee – no fee to drive around the park or hike the White House Trail. (All donations are welcomed.)

Directions: from Flagstaff, take 1-40 east and then Highway 191 north. The Visitor Center is 3 miles from Route 191 in Chinle, AZ.

NOTE: There are several businesses in the area that will offer Jeep tours and horseback riding or enlighten you with a journey inside the canyon by a certified private guide.

HILLTOP MOUNTAIN RUINS

TUZIGOOT NATIONAL MONUMENT

Another group of southern Sinagua people established their own community on the hilltops of the Verde Valley and other locations around the state. One of these places is Tuzigoot, which is Apache for "crooked water." These ruins are located twenty miles from Montezuma Castle and stretch along a crest above the Verde Valley. Tuzigoot was built from the natural resources found in the surrounding desert. Its massive cobblestone walls were uneven, two-to three-story dwellings, with approximately 110 rooms. There was a limited number of exterior doors and windows. The Sinagua would enter through a hole created in the roof of each pueblo. Living high on a hilltop in their rock apartments, they were well protected from the unforgiving desert climate and their enemies.

A small group of Sinagua first lived there for hundreds of years, until the 1200s, when the number of residents grew immensely. More rooms were added, but the people kept coming. Many of the farms outside the settlement were experiencing drought from a lack of water. Having nowhere else

Tuzigoot National Monument, Verde Valley, 2011.

A view of Tuzigoot walkway and visitor center, Verde Valley, 2011.

to go, they sought shelter amongst the cobblestone walls of Tuzigoot.

Like the Montezuma tribe, they were highly skilled in constructing canals for irrigation, growing corn, beans, squash, and cotton. Their communities also had many handmade tools, red-on-buff pottery, and ball courts resembling the Hohokam settlements. With all their clever building techniques, the mystery still remains why the Sinagua suddenly disappeared in the 1400s. Some feel that they may have used up their natural resources or maybe a plague or disease wiped them out, but since there is no written record, no one really knows.

Some Tuzigoot dwellings, Verde Valley, 2011.

Inside Tuzigoot restored two-story dwelling, Verde Valley, 2011.

Today, from the museum, visitors walk a path up the hill towards the ruins, which sit on forty-two acres. The signs with pictures provide an idea of what the small rooms may have looked like when the Sinagua Indians once lived there. There are only partial remains of the once-vast cobblestone walls. Some of the rooms have pits in the center, while others have Manos and mutates stones for grinding corn.

At the top of the hill, where the path circles around, sits the restored two-story dwelling. Inside of the space, an idea of what living in a 13th century Native American home was like is presented. The ceilings are low with wood beams securing them, and the floor is simply made of desert dirt. They've added stairs to walk up to the roof to take in the extraordinary scenery of the Verde Valley.

Tuzigoot from the top of two-story dwelling and part of the Verde Valley, 2011.

VISITOR INFORMATION

Website: www.nps.gov/tuzi

Phone: (928) 634-5564

Hours: open daily from 8 a.m. to 5 p.m.

Fees: collected in the park's Visitor Center; adults (16 and older) $5; children (under 16) free

Directions: Tuzigoot is 50 miles south of Flagstaff, Arizona, on U.S. Alt. 89 between Jerome and Sedona.

* All of the exhibits on display in the Visitor Center are recreations of how the Sinagua Indians survived and lived within the walls of Tuzigoot. In addition you will see many artifacts found at the site along with interactive computer programs.

Palatki Heritage site is over 600 years old and is located in the red rocks south of Sedona. Along with the ruins, there are hundreds of boulders marked with symbols that are said to have been etched over 6,000 years ago. This ancient Sinagua site has three separate paths that lead to the Palaki Heritage site. While one lone route guides visitors to the cliff dwellings, another guides to a place to observe the ruins, and a third trail arrives at a secluded place where the petroglyphs are found. All the footpaths are about one-quarter mile one way, an effortless walk, but not as simple for someone disabled.

Palatki has a sister locale, Honanki, and together they are the two most prevalent sites in the Red Rock area. Honanki means "Bear House" and Palatki means "Red House" in the Hopi language.

VISITOR INFORMATION

Websites: www.sedonahikingtrails.com/palatki-indian-ruins.html and www.sedona-verdevalley.com/attractionshighlights/palatkiheritagesite.html

Hours: open 7 days a week, 9:30 a.m. - 3 p.m.

Fees: a Red Rock pass (or equivalent) is mandatory for all vehicles parked at their cultural sites. You can acquire a pass at the site location.

Directions: to get to the Palatki site from Sedona, start by taking Highway 89A, which travels through West Sedona. Five miles beyond the last traffic light, make a right onto Forest Road 525; drive 5 miles to Forest Road 795 and another two miles until the parking lot of Palatki.

Another way: again, drive on Highway 89A and make a right onto Dry Creek Road. Look for the Palatki sign, which points to the site's location, and take the road until it ends. Then turn left onto Boynton Pass Road (FR 152C), take another left at the next stop sign, drive a couple more miles until you hit a gravel road and take that for three miles where you will turn right at the T intersection. From there, it is another two miles to Palatki.

If you are interested in hiking the cliff dwelling trail, the amount of visitors is limited to ten people at one time. Groups are scheduled every twenty minutes beginning at 9:40 a.m.

To make reservations, call (928) 282-3854 between 9:30 a.m. to 3 p.m..

REMNANTS OF THE HOHOKAM

History tells us that the Hohokam tribe migrated north from Mexico and settled in southern Arizona. The name Hohokam derives from the word "Hoohoogum," given to those living in that region of the Southwest desert and means, "Those who have gone." From the Hohokam ruins, it has been determined that they were a skilled group of farmers who built elaborate canals that went on for miles. Not much was known about this tribe nor written about their demise. We are able to study them through the well-engineered canals, ruins, and written stories on rocks, known as petroglyphs, which were left behind.

CASA GRANDE RUINS
NATIONAL MONUMENT

Casa Grande Ruins, Coolidge, 2012.

Casa Grande Ruins National Monument are located one hour southeast of Phoenix in Coolidge. These well-preserved remains are where the ancient Hohokam once lived. The main building, or Great House, is four stories high and sixty feet long. The first floor is on a mount and the walls are a mixture of a concrete-like combination of sand, clay, and calcium-carbonate or limestone. The Great House took 3,000 tons of Caliche mud that was layered resulting in the walls being four feet thick at the base and tapered towards the top. Anchored in the walls and used to form the ceilings were hundreds of juniper, pine, and fir trees they carried or floated sixty miles down the Gila River.

Massive walls of the Great House, Casa Grande Ruins, Coolidge, 2012.

The walls of the Great House face the four cardinal points of the compass and a circular hole in the upper west wall aligns with the setting sun at the summer solstice. The other holes in the walls each lined up with the sun and moon at specific times. It is a great mystery as to why the Hohokam built their structures to those exact measurements.

They were spiritual people who were often thankful for all the gifts nature gave them. Each night, the entire community would gather in the Great House and watch the setting sun through the small hole in the upper west side of the building.

One of the holes on the wall of the Great House, Casa Grande Ruins, 2012.

Surrounding the Great House were many other structures. These buildings were where the families of the village once lived. The walls were two- to three-feet thick and also formed from the same mixture that was used to construct the Great House. The open spaces

A couple of the smaller dwellings surrounding the Great House, Casa Grande Ruins, Coolidge, 2012.

were used for recreation and a market area where they sold their handmade goods. They also dug pits that were used as ball courts for playing games and having gatherings. This ancient civilization survived on the crops they grew, animals they hunted, and the natural plants they found in the surrounding desert. They had an abundant water source: the nearby Gila River.

Around the 1400s, the Hohokam people just seemed to fade away mysteriously. In 1694, when the Spanish missionaries discovered the Casa Grande ruins, it was just

Ball Court, Casa Grande Ruins, 2012.

Casa Grande Ruins Great House with metal cover to protect it, Coolidge, 2012.

a vacant structure. For two centuries, the ruins were pillaged by relic hunters and visitors curious around the site. In 1892, after years of trying to preserve the site, the Casa Grande Ruins were the first in the nation to become an archeological reserve.

Today, visitors often find that there is a feeling of eeriness surrounding the place.

Enter through the Visitor Center, pay a fee, and wander through the museum. Inside, see all the artifacts that were unearthed on the site, photos of the ruins in earlier years, and models of how their community may have appeared when the Hohokam lived there. Through the doors lies the main site where trails lead to the remnants of the grandiose ruins and where the populace once endured. While walking around the grounds, Native American flutes are resonating throughout, offering a peaceful feel to the location.

You can't help but notice the Great House, which is protected by the harsh sun with a large metal structure that covers the entire building. The walls in some areas have crumbled down, leaving openings for you to see inside. You can also see how thick the clay walls were and be amazed at the massive size of the four-story complex. The surrounding buildings are just half-walls giving a sense of the tiny quarters they used to live in.

Another path leads across the parking lot where a picnic area with shaded tables is located. Next to this space is an elevated structure to observe the site where a primeval ball court once existed. What used to serve as a recreation area some time ago is now just a dirt pit. Many mysteries and stories are still hidden amongst the thick walls of these amazing ruins.

Pottery and grinding stone in the museum and visitor center, Casa Grande ruins, Coolidge, 2012.

HOHOKAM PIMA NATIONAL MONUMENT

Snaketown are ruins situated near Sacaton and smack-dab in the middle of the Hohokam Pima National Monument. This site has unrivaled all other Hohokam settlements in the area. Digging started in the region in the 1930s by the Gila Pueblo Foundation and they continued to break ground in the 1960s. It appeared, by what they found, that an ancient tribe lived in the dwellings about 300 BC to 1050 AD. Two ball courts, a little pile where rituals were performed, a central plaza, and many living spaces (pithouses) for families and groups of people were unearthed. They figure that several thousand people may have lived in that community at one time. In 1964, it was listed as a National Historic Landmark and a National Monument in 1972. The site is owned by the Gila River Indian Community and, at the present time, Snaketown is not open to the public.

Mesa Grande is a huge Hohokam establishment found in Mesa. Findings revealed that this settlement probably existed from 1100 to 1450 AD. Digging was started at the site in the 1990s and excavation is continuing today. It appears that the site once crossed over 100 acres, but is now a small plot of land because of the growth in construction surrounding it. The site sits just west of the Mesa Hospital with mounds and well-preserved structures. A fence surrounds the area. It is on the Arizona Preservation Foundation's list of Most Endangered Historic Places.

VISITOR INFORMATION

Website: www.azmnh.org/arch/mesagrande.aspx

Address: 1000 N. Date Street (corner of Date and 10th Streets), Mesa, AZ 85201

Phone: (480) 644-3075 (Mesa Grande Visitor's Center)

Hours: 10 a.m. to 4 p.m. (Thursday and Friday); 11 a.m. to 4 p.m. (Saturday); 12 to 4 p.m. (Sunday); closed (Monday through Wednesday)

Fees: adults (12 and older) $5; children (3-12) $2

Mesa Grande Cultural Park
Website: http://azmnh.org/arch/mesagrande.aspx

FORTALEZA INDIAN RUINS

Fortaleza Indian Ruins are situated about forty-five miles southwest of Phoenix, near the town of Gila Bend. The name is Spanish for "Fort on a Hilltop" and the ruins sit alongside the north bank of the Gila River. The unmistakable fortress was built strong to stand up to what the desert elements had to offer. The Hohokam people lived in this community, which is located on the southwestern portion of the Hohokam terrain, around 1200 to 1450. It is thought that it may have taken the tribe over seventy-five years to complete the sixty rooms that inhabit the site. Time was not gentle to the ruins, and, throughout the years, people pillaging the artifacts and the harsh desert weather almost wiped it out of existence. In the 1960s, many of the walls were rebuilt using the same materials and floor plan the Hohokam used. In many other Hohokam sites, several artifacts were uncovered, but not so many in the Fortaleza location.

Mountains near Gila Bend, 2013.

Today, the Tohono O'odham Nation maintains that they are descendants of the Hohokam people and believe Fortaleza is a spiritual site. They used to allow people to visit the site with a permit, but no longer. Now it is forbidden for anyone to enter the area and they have posted "No Trespassing" signs. Perhaps in the future they will change their minds and let us enjoy the ruins once again.

GATLIN RUIN

Gatlin ruin is only a few miles from Fortaleza and near the Painted Rock Petroglyph site. This Hohokam village probably housed around 500 residents and was an important area for farming and trading goods. Gila Bend owns the Gatlin site and will add a cultural and educational park to the place.

VISITOR INFORMATION

The Town of Gila Bend

Website: www.gilabendaz.org

Address: 644 W. Pima Street, P.O. Box A, Gila Bend, AZ 85337

Phone: (928) 683-2255

MYSTERIES OF SEDONA

Sedona, 2012.

There are many ancient Native American ruins all over the state of Arizona. Many of these "houses of spirits" were built strong and we see the evidence in the partially found remains of their dwellings. From those ruins we get an understanding of how they survived. In central Arizona sits an entire mysterious city that many have referred to as being "spiritual." The city of Sedona spans, to some degree, into the Verde Valley, between Coconino and Yavapai counties. Surrounding the downtown are vivid orange-red sandstone rock creations as vibrant as Sedona's sunsets. There are many places to hike and enjoy the breathtaking scenery. People come to this serene settlement for the mountainous hiking trails, spiritual healing powers of the vortexes, and even for some UFO hunting. Sedona has it all.

The city was named after the wife of the first postmaster, Sedona Miller Schnebly, who was known for her generosity and sincerity.

One of the main characteristics of this town is its many vortexes, which seem to have New Age spiritual and healing abilities. Some are certain the organic formations of the red mountains are contributing factors to the energy of these soothing powers. It is believed that the energy comes from theoretical magnetically-charged routes inside the earth's

Hiking trail to vortexes in Sedona, 2012.

surface known as "ley lines." It is also thought that Sedona is one of the places where these lines intersect. In the 1950s, New Age enthusiast Page Bryant learnt about the vortexes through channeling. (Channeling is when a person falls into a deep tranquil state to communicate messages from a spiritual influence.) Sedona's vortexes are described as a "swirling center of subtle energy coming from the surface of the earth," which leave an insignificant quantity of lingering magnetism in areas where the energy is most predominant. If you meditate in the space where these vortexes are located, you can experience spiritual and sometimes even physical healing.

Sedona's vortexes have since become so popular that visitor centers now offer handouts and maps pointing out their locations. There are also guided tours that highlight Native American and New Age spirituality. One of the places I like to visit while in Sedona is the Center for the New Age. The building has four different shops offering massages, healings, psychic readings, vortex information, books, and crystals. In the back of one shop, you can have your aura read—I found that to be an interesting experience.

New Age Shops, Sedona, 2012.

Church of the Holy Cross, Sedona, 2012.

VISITOR INFORMATION

Center for the New Age

Website: http://sedonanewagestore.com

Address: 341 Hwy 179, Sedona, AZ 86336 (across from Tlaquepaque)

Phone: (928) 282-2085

Email: sedonanewage@gmail.com

Sedona is a wonderful place for hiking, camping, and taking jeep tours to some of the area's utmost remarkable sites. Hike some of the more famous rock formations around the city, such as Bell Rock, Cathedral Rock, and Lone Rock, to name a few. Visit the Chapel of the Holy Cross, a well-known and familiar site tucked inside the red rocks. This Roman Catholic cathedral was built in 1956 and took only eighteen months to complete. It offers spectacular views of Sedona and all its famous rock formations from its chapel's large windows.

Chapel of the Holy Cross

Website: www.redrockrealty.net/chapel.html

To get all the information you will need to make your hiking experience noteworthy, check out the following websites:

Sedona Arizona's Best Hiking Trails

http://bestsedonahiking.com

Great Sedona Hikes

www.greatsedonahikes.com

There are many places to camp and have a picnic amongst the red rocks of Sedona. The Forest Service provides information on all the locations in and around the Sedona area. Each place is usually on a "first-come, first-serve" basis with the exception of group sites. Some of the places will allow you to make a reservation, especially if you have a large group wanting to camp near each other.

Red Rock Country Camping and Picnicking

http://redrockcountry.org/recreation/camping.shtml

If hiking or camping does not excite you, perhaps a jeep ride through Sedona and the outskirts of the city sounds more like something you might enjoy. There are several different jeep tours that offer many diverse packages while on your thrill ride through the red rocks.

The Pink Jeep Tours

Website: http://pinkjeeptours.com/sedona/our-tours

The Pink Jeep Tours have been taking people on tours of Sedona and others places since 1960. They drive paths and jaunt through the back roads where you can experience places you wouldn't see in your own car. They offer several different deals and an essential tour to add to your trip to Sedona.

Jeep from the "Pink Jeep Tours," Sedona, 2012

Sedona Off Road Adventures

Website: www.sedonajeeptours.com

Sedona Off Road Adventures offers you another tour option. They will present you with a safe and naturally exhilarating ride through all the historical sites and amazing scenery. Check them out and see what type of deals they have to offer.

A Day in the West Jeep Tours

Website: www.adayinthewest.com
A Day in the West Jeep Tours provides you with a breathtaking ride back in time through the history of the red rock city. If you want a fun Wild West experience, then this is the tour for you. Like the other jeep outings, this tour has its own unique daily packages as well.

If the jeep tours are not enough and you would like a different kind of experience, try a UFO tour. Sedona UFO Sky Tours will take you to some of the city's UFO hotspots and provide you with equipment to make your adventure most successful. With the night-vision goggles and binoculars, your vision of the clear Sedona nights afford you the opportunity of a better view to see the UFOs. You will sit near a vortex and feel its energy while basking in the splendor of the starry skies.

UFO Sky Tours

Website: www.sedonaufoskytours.com

Phone: (805) 815-8989

Email: info@SedonaUFOSkyTours.com

Hours: Meet at dusk at The Encounter Sedona Storefront; 1385 89A, West Sedona

Nighttime Fee: adults – $75; children (12 and under) free; cash only please

* Next to the Old Sedona Bar and Grill. The tour is usually 1.5 to 2 hours.

The Center for the New Age also provides UFO tours. They will set you up with equipment to help in spotting UFOs and take you to some of the best places around for hunting our visitors in the sky. Check out their website for information. http://sedonanewagestore.com/sedona-visitors/ufo-tours

Alien statues above New Age Shops, Sedona, 2012.

Entrance to Tlaquepaque, Sedona, 2012.

The astounding scenery of Sedona is not all this city can bestow upon you. There are many accommodations for your shopping and dining pleasure. One of the places you must see while visiting Sedona, Arizona, is Tlaquepaque (*Tia-keh-pah-keh*). The name means "best of everything" and it was built in the 1970s. Located near Oak Creek with flourishing vegetation all around its grounds, Tlaquepaque has the look of an original Mexican town. Inside are many interesting shops, galleries, and restaurants with cobble-stoned walkways and arched entryways with vines growing all over the stucco walls.

VISITOR INFORMATION

Website: www.tlaq.com

Address: 336 State Route 179, Sedona, AZ 86339

Phone: (928) 282-4838

Email: info@tlaq.com

Hours: 10 a.m. to 5 p.m. (shops) open daily; restaurant hours vary (closed Christmas and Thanksgiving)

Uptown Sedona is located in the center of town where Highway 89A and 179 come together. Along the half-mile route, you can find many diverse shops, restaurants, and cafés. Below the shopping locality run the cool waters of Oak Creek. Amongst the various assorted shops are Native American and Southwest items, galleries that display local artists' works, and many of the touring establishments. Be sure to park your car and take a stroll through Uptown Sedona.

VISITOR INFORMATION

Website: www.sedonacentralreservations.com/shop-uptown-sedona.aspx

COFFEE POT RESTAURANT

Coffee Pot Rock, Sedona, 2012.

Sedona has many places to dine, and some more quirky than others. The Coffee Pot Restaurant is located near the Coffee Pot Rock. It has been in business since the 1950s and offers around 101 different omelets for your enjoyment. They provide breakfast all day long and serve it with the best-tasting coffee. It also serves many other delicious meals at affordable prices. The service is just as wonderful as the food. There is additionally a small shop with various items.

VISITOR INFORMATION

Website: www.coffeepotsedona.com

Address: 2050 West Highway 89A (just west of Coffee Pot Road), Sedona, AZ 86336

Phone: (928) 282-6626

Hours: open daily for breakfast and lunch from 6 a.m. to 2 p.m.

RED PLANET DINER

Outside Red Planet Diner, Sedona, 2012.

Red Planet Diner is one of those places that should be experienced while in Sedona. This odd diner caters to the UFO lover with its out-of-this-world décor. From its location, the diner is treated to the outstanding views of Sedona's red rocks and scenery. They also boast to having the best burgers in town. My friend and I gave this place a try and loved it.

VISITOR INFORMATION

Website: www.redplanetdiner.net

Address: 1655 W. State Route 89A, Sedona, AZ 86336

Phone: (928) 282-6070

After you spent the day touring, shopping, and eating, you will need a nice place to lay your head for the night. Sedona has many hotels, resorts, and cabins to choose from. The prices range from affordable to extravagant, depending on what type of staying experience you are looking for. Places are located in varied areas around the state and provide you with amazing views of the mountains or Oak Creek. Some offer massages and other packages to make your stay more comfortable.

L'AUBERGE DE SEDONA

L'Auberge De Sedona is a resort with hotel rooms and cottages that sit along the creek. I had the pleasure of staying there with my husband in one of their cottages. Not only is the place near the serine waters, but it is just below Uptown Sedona as well. We also dined at their restaurant and sat near the creek listening to the sounds of the cool waters rushing by us. It was very romantic.

L'Auberge de Sedona Resort, Sedonia, 2012.

VISITOR INFORMATION

Website: www.lauberge.com

Address: 301 Little Lane, Sedona, AZ 86336

Phone: (928) 282-1661

King's Ransom is located near places to shop and eat, and the prices are affordable. I have stayed here during urban exploring road trips and had an excellent experience.

VISITOR INFORMATION

Website:
www.kingsransomsedona.com

Address: 771 Hwy 179, Sedona, AZ 86336

Phone: (928) 282-7151

Hotels, Resorts and Cabins
www.visitsedona.com

OAK CREEK CANYON

I can't talk about Sedona and all its wonders without mentioning Oak Creek Canyon. This breathtaking ravine is located near Sedona and south of Flagstaff. One of the Grand Canyon's little sisters, this picturesque valley of trees, red rocks, and wandering creek is a site to be appreciated. From Flagstaff, there is a beautiful scenic overpass where many Native Americans have tables displaying their handmade goods for sale. After taking in the beauty of the canyon, it is time to drive the winding roads

Oak Creek and Oak Creek
Canyon, 2011.

and U-shaped turns to reach the bottom of the canyon. It is approximately thirteen miles from the lookout to Sedona, but there are places to stop along the way.

Slide Rock State Park

One of those places along the route is Slide Rock State Park. I have visited this place many times throughout my years as a child and an adult. Slide Rock got its name from the natural water slide formed by the slippery bed of Oak Creek. It is located in Oak Creek Canyon and only seven miles from Sedona.

In 1907, Frank L. Pendley developed the land and obtained a title under the Homestead Act in 1910. He created an irrigation system that watered his apple orchard. The road through the canyon was finished in 1914 and Pendley took advantage of the traffic and built the tourists cabins for them to rent.

On July 10, 1985, the Arizona State Parks acquired the park and, two years later, Slide Rock State Park was dedicated. On December 23, 1991, the Pendley Homestead Historic District was placed on the National Register of Historic Places. Pendley's apple farm is still maintained today.

VISITOR INFORMATION

Website:
http://azstateparks.com/Parks/SLRO

Address: 6871 West Highway 89A, Sedona, AZ 86336

Phone: (928) 282-3034

Hours: 8 a.m. to 6 p.m. (spring); 8 a.m. to 7 p.m. (summer)

Fees: $10 per vehicle (up to 4 adults, 14 years or older), each extra adult is $3

* No pets allowed or to be left in vehicles. Also, bring a few pairs of pants because the smooth rocks on the slide will wear holes in your drawers.

There are several places to picnic along Oak Creek as well as places to camp. You can pitch a tent, roll out your RV, or rent one of the several cabins located inside the canyon. No matter where you stop in Oak Creek Canyon, the views are to die for.

Sedona/Oak Creek Campgrounds
Websites: http://camprrm.com/2009/08/sedona-oak-creek-canyon-campgrounds and www.sedonahappy.com/sedona-camping.html

Slide Rock, Oak Creek Canyon, 1990.

Briar Patch Inn
(Warm and comfy cabins in Oak Creek)

Website: www.briarpatchinn.com

There are many more places that offer you a cabin and cottage stay while in Sedona and Oak Creek Canyon. The following website has all the information you will need for make your Sedona stay an enjoyable one.

Sedona Chamber of Commerce and Visitor Center

Website: www.visitsedona.com/article/73

NATIVE AMERICAN PETROGLYPHS

Petroglyphs at Painted Rock, Northwest Gila Bend, 2013.

Petroglyphs have been found on rocks and boulders all over the Southwest. A petroglyph is an ancient drawing carved by primordial man. They are pictogram and logogram images done by wearing down or chafing impressions in solid rock. Some say they are astronomical markers, maps, or some type of symbolic communication telling stories of life many centuries ago. This ancient rock art is one way to study how the pre-Columbian civilizations may have once lived and where they mysteriously disappeared to.

Painted Rock entrance sign, 2013.

Painted Rock Petroglyph Site is one of the many locations found in Arizona and is eighteen miles west by northwest of Gila Bend on the Painted Rock Mountains. This site has over 800 images that are engraved into basalt boulders. Many of the imprints can be found on the eastern side of the mountain's rim.

Other people who have come upon this site have left their mark on the boulders, too. Along with the petroglyphs, and dotted throughout

Painted Rock, 2013

the landscape, are traces of ancient Hohokam ruins. Some historical and famous events happened in close proximity of the site, such as Juan Bautisa de Anza's journey. He originated the city of San Francisco expedition. In 1989, the Painted Rock Petroglyph Site became under the authority of the Bureau of Land Management.

Along with the several hundred etchings, the area also supplies picnic tables and barbeque grills under covered verandas. Near the picnic area, the site has a small building where the restrooms are provided. There are no places for trailers to attach to electricity, no water for drinking, or a place to dump your waste. If you want to camp there, you will have to basically rough it. However, not far away, in Gila Bend, is a campground with all the amenities you will need to make your camping experience rewarding if you choose less primitive conditions.

Picnic area at painted Rock, 2013.

Petroglyphs found at Painted Rock, 2013.

VISITOR INFORMATION

Address: Rocky Point Road, Dateland, AZ 85333

Phone: (623) 580-5500

Directions: from Gila Bend, travel 12.5 miles west on Interstate 8 to the Painted Rock Dam Road (Exit 102). Head north for 10.7 miles of paved road to Rocky Point Road, which is a dirt road. Turn west for about 0.6 miles to the Painted Rock Petroglyph Site.

* The best time to see the petroglyphs is during the months of October to April. The other months may be too hot, plus rattlesnakes and other poisonous beings are usually seen roaming around the boulders. They do have signs as a reminder to be careful. For more information on the site, contact:

Lower Sonoran Field Office

Address: 21605 N. 7th Avenue, Phoenix, AZ 85027-2929

Phone: (623) 580-5500

Hours: 7:30 a.m. to 4:15 p.m., Monday to Friday

One of the most prevalent sites with petroglyphs is located in the Verde Valley between Sedona and Flagstaff. The V-Bar-V Heritage Site is well preserved and was obtained by the Coconino National Forest in 1994. The location has approximately 1,032 etchings on 13 panels and is a wealth of information about the beliefs in each era of the Hohokam people's existence. The distinctive approach of the drawings is identified as the "Beaver Creek Rock Art Style" used by the southern Sinagua between 1150 AD and 1400.

A visitor center and bookstore are located near the parking lot on premises. The Red Rock Heritage website provides updated information regarding tour and guides, which are arranged by a couple of different groups.

VISITOR INFORMATION

Directions: the V-Bar-V Heritage Site is located 2.8 miles east of the I-17 and SR179 (FR618) highways. The entrance is on the right, less than one-half miles past the Beaver Creek Campground.

Hours: 9:30 a.m. to 3 p.m. (entrance gate closes at 3 p.m.); Fridays, Saturdays, Sundays, and Mondays; closed Thanksgiving and Christmas

Fees: a Red Rock Pass (or equivalent) required for all vehicles parked at the social sites. Passes can be bought at any of the sites during regular business hours.

* No pets allowed at any of the petroglyph sites.

Red Rock Heritage Sites

www.redrockcountry.org

Address: P.O. Box 20429, Sedona AZ 86341

Phone: (928) 282-3854

ROCK ART RANCH

VISITOR INFORMATION

Owner: Brantley Baird

Address: Box 224, Joseph City, AZ 86032

Phone: (928) 288-3260

Fees: Inquire when you call

Rock Art Ranch is privately owned near Winslow with a chasm full of petroglyphs. The profound gorge has a brook flowing inside its mighty walls and stairs leading inside the ravine along the rim to an observation area built by the ranch's owner. This space has an incredible view and is a nice place to have a picnic. The ranch also has a museum for your pleasure.

Entrance to White Tank Mountain Regional Park, 2011.

White Tank Mountain Regional Preserve mountain range is located west of Phoenix near the city of Surprise. The range gets its name for the white granite near the base of the mountains and its many depressions, also known as "tanks." It is believed that the range was formed about 30 million years ago by earthquake activities and detaching from a fault line. Although the peaks of each range are approximately the same altitude, the tallest is the Barry Goldwater Peak at 4,083 feet. The rocky terrain is beautiful, but dangerous. The mountain range consists of jagged ridges and bottomless canyons where, after a rainfall, water will build up and run swiftly down the sheer canyons.

In the mountains, the White Tank Mountain Regional Park is an area where many like to visit and hike. Many of the locations in this park are undeveloped wilderness with varied indigenous species roaming around the desert grounds. The mountain range has numerous petroglyphs found scattered around the peaks and may predate the Hohokam people. Approximately eleven archaeological sites were recognized, along with seven Hohokam villages. There are various trails leading to these sites and villages dispersed and marked for your interests. Take as many pictures of the sites and petroglyphs as you like, but all they ask is that you don't touch them.

VISITOR INFORMATION

Website: www.maricopa.gov/parks/white_tank/

Address: 20304 W. White Tank Mountain Road, Waddell, AZ 85355

Phone: (623) 935-2505

Email: whitetankpark@mail.maricopa.gov

Petroglyphs at South Mountain Park, Phoenix, 2011.

South Mountain Park is just south of Phoenix and is another place to find petroglyphs. This park is about 1,600 acres and has several different trails where etchings can be found. Also carved by the ancient Hohokam people, the drawings are believed by the Pima Indians as having a mystical importance. No one really knows exactly what this prehistoric tribe was thinking when each drawing was carved.

VISITOR INFORMATION

Website: www.phoenix.gov/PARKS/ southmnt.html

Address: (Main Entrance) 10919 S. Central Avenue, Phoenix, AZ 85042

Phone: (602) 534-6324

Hours: 5 a.m. to 7 p.m. (for all trailhead areas); after 7 p.m., the entrance gates will be closed.

* Trails remain open until 11 p.m.

Near the park entrance and behind the closed Education Center is the Judith Tunnel Accessible Trail. This trail is rather effortless to hike with the petroglyphs located about a quarter-mile from the start. You will see a covered veranda near the area where the boulders with the engraved drawings can be found.

Behind the visitor's center is the Holbert Trail. This path is tricky, with sharp rocks that take you down a little valley. It is a bit more challenging than the other trails. This arduous task is worth it when you see all the amazing petroglyphs etched on the boulders.

There are only a couple of the trails found on South Mountain that lead to the location of petroglyphs.

Sign for the Holbert Trail on South Mountain, Phoenix, 2011.

Petroglyphs at South Mountain Park, Phoenix, 2011.

CHAPTER 2

Hell for Gold and Squandered Wealth

Vulture Mine, 2011.

These towns may be small, but the stories from their historic past are as rich now as they once were. Arizona mining towns, at one time, were bustling with excitement, but now are considered ghost towns. Why would people bring their families to these places in the Arizona Territory with the threat of Indian attacks, overbearing heat, and lack of water? The minerals found in the dry soil, such as gold, silver, and copper, drew the money-hungry opportunists. Some braved the unknown in hopes of a better life for their families. Whatever their reasons, a town located near a successful mine flourished. During their heyday, every town hit its peak of inhabitants who lived in wood or brick structures and enjoyed the wealth the mines brought them.

Today, these once-booming mining towns are all but abandoned with only a handful of people to still call them home. The towns are surviving from the many tourists who are interested in the history, wanting a Wild West experience, or to check out the rumors of the many ghosts that still seem to live in these small desert settlements.

VULTURE MINE
(A DEAD MAN'S PLAYGROUND)

Entrance to Vulture Mine and trails, 2011.

Hanging Tree, Vulture Mine, 2011.

If you travel about seventy miles north of Phoenix and approximately fifteen miles southwest of Wickenburg, you will find the ghost town of Vulture City. This once-booming mining town now sits empty with many of the still-standing structures slowly decaying with time. Underneath its dirt floors lay the many bones of those who crossed the wrong person and was buried right where they died. This "dead man's playground" is rumored to be haunted by ghosts and is an astonishing walk back into Arizona's most colorful past.

The history of this unlikely town is associated with a man named Henry Wickenburg. He was an Austrian prospector who, in 1863, discovered a quartz deposit containing gold in the middle of the Arizona desert. He later sold his deposit to Benjamin Phelps, who was acting on behalf of a group of investors known as the Vulture Mining Company.

By the 1890s, the population of their little mining town, called Vulture City, grew to over 5,000 men, women, and children. The Vulture Mines were flourishing, which not only attracted families, but also the insatiable opportunists. Soon the town became unsafe for those living there. All the minerals found in the mine were kept in a vault under the Assay Office. Although there were two guards on duty watching the safe, many bandits, Indians, and other greedy bastards attacked the place constantly. With over $200,000 in gold removed from the mine and stored under the Assay Office, the outlaws got restless. By the 1930s, the monetary worth of $200,000 was a massive amount. At today's prices, that sum would exceed over 200 million dollars. Because of all the gold extracted from Vulture Mine, it became the most industrious mine in Arizona history.

Life in Vulture City became unbearable for many, especially those with families. Countless people were afraid to leave the perimeter of the town for fear of their lives. Inside the town's borders, the murder and rape cases were all too frequent. There were no lawyers or trials in Vulture City. Anyone convicted of a crime was either hanged by a vigilante committee or buried right where they were killed. By 1942, President Franklin Roosevelt closed the mine because of World War II, with a promise to the people that it would only be for six months. Unfortunately, Vulture Mine was never reopened and the settlement quickly became nothing but a ghost town.

Remnants of Vulture Mine equipment, 2011.

Today, Vulture Mine lies empty with scattered and decaying, abandoned structures throughout the area. Start your tour at Vulture's Roost, which is also the museum. Behind the building is a path to the first stop on the main street, the Assay Office. This building is too unsafe for curious visitors to roam around inside and has a wire fence around it. Next is the bordello where unsavory dealings happened on a daily basis. Also, on the main street are a kitchen/dining building and other structures that are barely standing. The next stop is the Glory Hole and main entrance to the mine shaft. The

Machine Shop and Ball Mill Power Plant, Vulture Mine, 2011.

Assay Office, Vulture Mine, 2011.

hole has a 35 percent slope and drops around 2,100 feet with wood planks nailed over the entrance to shield visitors from harm. Also at the entrance is a concrete slab marking Henry Wickenburg's first strike, along with a grandiose wood head frame.

A path behind the blacksmith's shop leads to the machine shop and Ball Mill Power Plant, which are located on a hill south of Main Street. Each building still has the equipment and machines that powered the mines in its heyday. The Ball Mill building at one time housed large steel balls that compressed debris and low-grade ore. They now sit rusty and broken as a powerful reminder of how much the mine in times past thrived. Outside the mine's entrance are scattered rusty items that once were used in obtaining the minerals from the mine. The trail circles around the perimeter to Henry Wickenburg's original home, the hanging tree, bunkhouses, a jail, and hotels. The schoolhouse can be found on the other side of town.

Even today, some believe that this "dead man's playground" is full of bodies buried in the dry and dusty dirt. They feel that the spirits of the miners seem to be hanging around and still protecting the gold. Paranormal groups investigating the mines have reported rocks being thrown at them through windows and hearing footsteps and disembodied voices.

VISITOR INFORMATION

Vulture Mine's new owners have opened the town for tours, but only at specific days and hours. Check the Wickenburg Chamber of Commerce website below for days and times.

Vulture Mine has a shop at Vulture's Roost. After you visit and tour Vulture Mine, stop by the nearby city of Wickenburg. There you will enjoy the sites of the historic downtown area, quaint shops, and cafes. Stop by the Wickenburg Chamber of Commerce for all the information.

Wickenburg Chamber of Commerce

Website:
www.WickenburgChamber.com

Address: 216 N. Frontier Street, Wickenburg, AZ 85390

Phone: (928) 684-5479 or 1(800) 942-5242

GLOBE
(PLACE OF METAL)

Old Dominion Mine, Globe, 2011.

In 1873, the Anderson brothers dug out of the earth a silver nugget with a globe-like shape and named their claim the "Globe Mine" after their treasure. Three years later, in 1876, a small mining camp was founded and was named "Globe" after the Anderson's mine, which was located nearby. By the 1900s, the silver deposits were drying up, but more copper was being discovered in its place. During this time, Globe's Old Dominion Mine, which opened in 1881, became one of the richest mines in the world. Because of the large abundance of copper, the tiny mining camp began to grow. Globe was now considered a town with retail shops, banks, a newspaper company, and a stage linking it to Silver City, New Mexico.

On December 22, 1877, the Globe post office was opened. By 1881, the town grew so large it officially became the City of Globe.

Globe enjoyed all the popularity and riches that the Old Dominion Mine was bringing this remarkable little city. Along with the extraordinary past came a sordid one as well. Globe's history is marked with murders, stagecoach robberies, outlaws, lynching, and Apache raids. Such names as Geronimo, Apache Kid, Ike Clanton, and Phineas Clanton are forever linked with this city. The Clanton brothers ended up in Globe after the gunfight at the O.K. Corral. Phineas ended up hanging his hat in Globe until his death in 1906. When he was finally captured, the Apache Kid's trial was held at the Globe Courthouse. After he was convicted of his crimes, he was taken to the Arizona Territorial Prison in Yuma by Sheriff Glenn Reynolds.

Globe has been hit hard by the mines closing and the merciless economy. The population has dwindled over the years and many businesses have closed their doors in the historic district. Even though the town has been devastated, there are still reasons to visit Globe. In the historic district, you will find antique shops and great places to eat. Since the city has lots of history, there are many places to tour and take in the sights.

VISITOR INFORMATION

The Old Dominion Mine is now open for tours and can be seen from the highway. You will be able to hike the trails and check out the new amenities. There are plans to open more of the mine with various other attractions.

The Gila County Historic Museum is another place to see while in Globe. This wonderful place has photos, artifacts, and other information on the history of Globe.

Gila County Historic Museum

Address: 1330 N. Broad Street, Globe, AZ 85001

Phone: (928) 425-7385

Open: Monday to Friday

Also visit and tour the Gila County Courthouse and Jail. Both places have many Wild West photos and artifacts from Globe's interesting past. Outside, between the two buildings and above the ground, is the metal bridge where prisoners would walk to the jail after being sentenced in the courthouse.

Gila County Courthouse

Address: 1400 E. Ash Street, Globe, AZ 85501

Phone: (928) 425-3231

Gila County Jail: Globe

Address: 1100 S. South Street, Globe, AZ 85501

Phone: (928) 425-4449

Globe Courthouse, Globe, 2011.

Old Globe Jail, Globe, 2011.

NOFTSGER HILL INN

A great place to lay your head for a night or two is at the Noftsger Hill Inn. This building once was an elementary school and sits high atop a hill overlooking Globe. Today, it has been remodeled and converted into an impressive bed and breakfast. Inside, you will see lots of evidence of the old schoolhouse with class-size rooms, high ceilings, large windows, and in some rooms, original chalkboards still hang on the walls. Included in the price with your night's stay is a delicious homemade breakfast. Also, if you like sleeping with ghosts, this is your kind of inn. My friends and I have had some paranormal experiences while staying there.

Website: www.noftsgerhillinn.com

Address: 425 North Street, Globe, AZ 85501

Phone: (928) 425-2260 or toll free 1 (877) 780-2479

Directions: To get to Globe from Phoenix, AZ, drive up U.S. Highway 60 (Historic Old West Highway). Globe is along the highway, about 90 minutes east of Phoenix.

AUTHOR NOTE

Another place I highly recommend while you are in Globe is the Besh-Ba-Gowah ancient ruins at the edge of town. I dedicated an entire section to this place in Chapter 1, "House of the Spirits." Also, there are many abandoned places all around Globe for the urban explorer to photograph.

Noftsger Hill Inn, Globe, 2011.

Inside one room of the Noftsger Hill Inn, Globe, 2011.

BISBEE
(QUEEN OF THE COPPER CAMPS)

Downtown Historic Bisbee, 2010.

Snuggled below U.S. Highway 80, and 82 miles southeast of Tucson, is the historic old town of Bisbee. Like many of the mining towns in Arizona, Bisbee was first founded because a rich vein of minerals was discovered nearby. It was in 1877 when a civilian tracker named Jack Dunn lead a small group of soldiers into the Mule Mountains. This band of military men was on the hunt for unruly Apaches reported in the area. To their surprise, instead of finding Apache warriors, they stumbled across signs of mineral deposits consisting of lead, copper, and silver. Shortly afterwards, a claim on the mine was filed and the town of Bisbee was born.

Word spread quickly of the wealthy find in the Mule Mountains and, soon, many traveled to the Arizona Territory in hopes of striking it rich. With so many claims being submitted, the small town of Bisbee was given the nickname "Queen of the Copper Camps."

The population grew rapidly and all the men, women, and children who called Bisbee home were lacking in basic needs. They worked diligently on improving medical care and fire protection, along with better sanitation and cleaner water. On January 9, 1902, Bisbee grew in numbers and the town became the City of Bisbee. By 1910, the city was the largest in the territory with a population of over 25,000 people. The mine was pumping out over 8 billion pounds of copper, 102 million ounces of silver, and 2.8 million ounces of gold, along with millions of pounds of zinc, lead, and manganese. This growth also brought about a change in the Cochise County seat, moving it from Tombstone to Bisbee in 1929.

For several decades, Bisbee enjoyed the prosperity the abundant mines were producing. By 1974, the funds for the mines had been exhausted, resulting in the closing of all mining operations a year later. Many of the residents, miners, and businessmen left for other places, hoping to find a life Bisbee could no longer provide. Houses and other buildings were left empty with only memories living between the quiet walls.

Today, with the inexpensive real estate, ideal weather, and an extraordinary history,

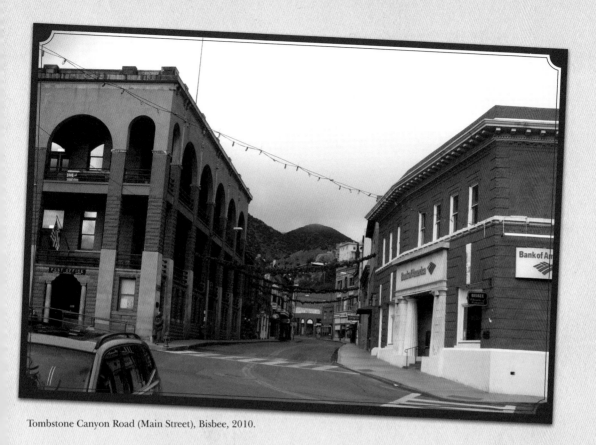

Tombstone Canyon Road (Main Street), Bisbee, 2010.

A view of historic Bisbee from the park, Bisbee, 2012.
Courtesy of Mike Brieddy.

Bisbee 1000, The Great Stair Climb, Bisbee,
2012. *Courtesy of Mike Brieddy.*

Bisbee has attracted various types of people who call it home. This unusual mix of hippies, retirees, investors, and artists are among the residents living in this quirky mining town. There are many homes that sit high above Tombstone Canyon Road of old historic Bisbee. From the street below, some of the houses have hundreds of stairs leading to their front doors. Some of the structures are empty and are in need of repair, but some have been restored to their former glory by the people living in them now.

The architecture and history of Bisbee has been refurbished and is kept well preserved, which is apparent when you walk along Tombstone Canyon Road. The historic buildings lining the street are filled with antique, New Age, and other unique shops. There are plenty of places to eat, drink, and satisfy your sweet tooth along the way. At night, the streets are dark and eerie, but the saloons and bars are lively with local entertainment. If you plan to spend a night or two in Bisbee, the town offers several hotels and inns for your sleeping and dining pleasure. The astonishing history and the many claims of paranormal activity are some of the reasons this small mining town has survived throughout all the hardships time has thrust upon it.

VISITOR INFORMATION

City of Bisbee

Websites: www.cityofbisbee.com and www.discoverbisbee.com

Address: 118 Arizona Street, Bisbee, AZ 85603

Queen Mine Tour

Website: www.queenminetour.com

Address: 478 Dart Road (south of Old Historic Bisbee exit), Bisbee, AZ 85603

Phone: (520) 432-2071 or toll free 1 (866) 432-2071

Tour times: 9 a.m., 10:30 a.m., noon, 2 p.m., 3:30 p.m.

Tour rates: adults (12 and older) $13; children (4-12) $5.50; children (under 4) free. Prices subject to change

HOTELS, INNS, BED AND BREAKFASTS:

Copper Queen Hotel

Website: www.copperqueen.com

Address: 11 Howell Avenue, Bisbee, AZ 85603

Phone: (520) 432-2216

Rates: low season – from $89 to $129; high season – from $122 to $177

Copper Queen Hotel, Bisbee, 2010.

This hotel was built in 1902 by the wealthy Copper Queen Mining Company. It was first constructed for the mining camp executives and played host to traveling men, governors, and dignitaries. I have personally stayed here a couple of times and enjoyed my stay. I love how the furnishings in each room, sitting areas, and lobby are decorated in the 1920s era. We liked spending time in the bar at night and consuming a delicious breakfast in the restaurant in the morning. My friends and I were drawn to this place because of the many ghost stories. We were not disappointed.

Oliver House (B&B Hotel)

Website: www.discoverbisbee.com

Address: 24 Sowles Avenue, Bisbee, AZ 85603

Phone: (520) 432-1900

Email: parkerhill40@yahoo.com

Rates: $75-$97 per night

The Oliver House is located in the historic district and was built in 1909 by Edith Ann Oliver, wife of Henry Oliver (a mining tycoon). This twelve-room house was originally used as mine offices and later became a boarding house for miners. It has a history of murder and violence.

Oliver House, Bisbee, 2010.

Inn at Castle Rock

Website: www.theinnatcastlerock.com

Address: 112 Tombstone Canyon Road, Bisbee, AZ 85603

Phone: (520) 432-4449 (for room rates, details, and reservations)

Rates: Rooms start at $89 per night, double occupancy.

The inn is located in downtown old Bisbee at the foot of Castle Rock. It was built in 1895 and was called the Muirhead House, named after Bisbee's first mayor, John Joseph Muirhead. This building was the largest wood structure in Bisbee and used as a boarding house for miners. In 1948, the place was turned into apartments until the 1980s when Jim Babcock bought the place. By 2007, it was shut down and left abandoned. Two years later, Chris Brown bought it, changed the name to the Inn at Castle Rock, and renovated it with plans to restore it back to its former glory.

Inn at Castle Rock, Bisbee, 2010.

Bisbee has many other places to lay your hat while spending a night or two in town. To see all this town has to offer check out the Greater Bisbee Chamber of Commerce website:

www.bisbeearizona.com
or call (520) 432-5421.

JEROME
(HILLTOP GHOST TOWN)

Historic District, Jerome, 2011.

If you are traveling west along Interstate 89 ALT, about twenty miles from Sedona, you will end up in the quaint little settlement of Jerome. This copper mining town was built on Cleopatra Hill near Prescott and founded in 1876. After three prospectors laid claim to the copper deposits they found, the mining camp known as Jerome was born. In 1883, the men sold their rights to the United Verde Copper Company for a tidy sum. Shortly afterwards, the mining camp grew, with wood and canvas shacks lining the hills near the mines. Later, the mining camp was bustling with all sorts of people wanting to strike it rich. The camp

grew into a town and was named after Eugene Jerome, who was the principle backer. Two years later, the company shut down because the cost of operations became too much. A new owner, William A. Clark, took over and added a narrow gauge railroad to reduce freight costs.

By the 20th century, the United Verde was the largest producing copper mine in the Arizona Territory. The canvas cabins no longer existed and were replaced by brick and framed buildings. Jerome now had churches, schools, theatres, hotels, shops, a civic center, and was the place where many wanted to live. This mining town was made up of many different

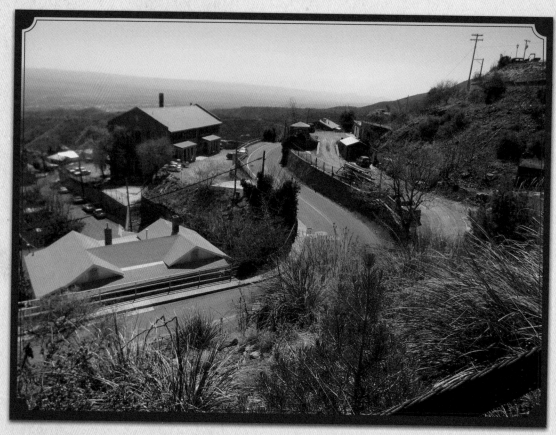

Winding roads through Jerome, 2011.

characteristics of people seeking riches from the mines below. The international blend of people made life in Jerome stimulating and energetic. People continued to move to this booming town hoping for work and a better life.

By 1916, and with the addition of the Little Daisy Mine, Jerome was pumping out copper from two separate mines. The investors and financiers were enjoying all the profits the mines were producing. During this era, Jerome was the fourth largest city in the Arizona Territory. Over 3 million pounds of copper was being extracted from the mines through the narrow underground passages.

Living in Jerome wasn't always easy. The town was hit with countless fires destroying several structures each time. They always rebuilt, but were faced with other unsafe situations living on a hillside had to offer. Because the mountainside had a thirty-degree slope, some of the buildings slid down the incline. To the delight of some of the people, one of the buildings was the town's jail. By 1918, with several fires in the mine's tunnels and the constant dynamiting, which caused the ground to shift and cracking in many of the buildings, the mines took an enormous beating. In 1935, Phelps-Dodge took over the United

Bartlett Hotel, Jerome, 2011.

Mile High Grill & Inn and Town Hall located in downtown Jerome, 2011.

Verde, and three years later, in 1938, the Little Daisy Mine shut down for good. With the prices of copper continuously falling, and the loss of profits, Jerome's copper mines shut down.

Jerome's peek in population hit 15,000 in 1929, but dropped down to 50 souls living there by the late 1950s. Today, the peaceful community is thriving, thanks to the writers, artists, musicians, historians, and families who call Jerome home. Interstate 89 ALT narrows down to two lanes and leads up the hill to the town of Jerome. The road weaves amongst the historic buildings, giving the feeling of having been taken back in time. Many of the old structures have been restored by the residents who either live in them or use them for shops, restaurants, museums, or hotels.

There are many historic places to see while in Jerome. One interesting place in the area is called the "Cribs District," which is located across from the English Kitchen, in the back alley of the buildings and was once part of Jerome's "prostitution row." Urban explorers and ghost hunters can find plenty abandoned structures, haunted bed and breakfasts, or ghostly hotels. Jerome is known as the "largest ghost town in America."

VISITOR INFORMATION

HOTELS AND BED AND BREAKFASTS

Jerome Grand Hotel

Website: www.jeromegrandhotel.com

Address: 200 Hills Street, Jerome, AZ 86331

Phone: (928) 634-8200

Jerome Grand Hotel, Jerome, 2011.

This grandiose hotel was first built as a hospital in 1926 and named United Verde Hospital. It was outfitted with all the latest equipment and was the most prepared hospital in all of Arizona. In 1950, when the mines dried up and many of the people left, the hospital was forced to close its doors. The building stood abandoned for more than forty-four years until it was bought, renovated, and renamed the Jerome Grand Hotel. The hotel opened in 1997 and is a magnificent place to stay and take in the breathtaking views of Jerome and the Verde Valley.

Ghost City Inn (Bed and Breakfast)

Website: www.ghostcityinn.com

Address: 541 Main Street (Hwy. 89A), Jerome, AZ 86331

Phone: (928) 634-4678

Email: ghostcityinn@msn.com

This quaint little B&B can be found in the heart of the town. It was built around 1890 and was first used as accommodations for middle mine management. The place has seen many different owners and uses. It was once a funeral home, art gallery, boarding house, an ashram, and now an inn. It was restored in 1994 and the current owners have refurbished all of the rooms. The rooms range from $105 to $155 per night plus tax.

Connor Hotel

Website: www.connorhotel.com

Address: 164 Main Street (Hwy. 89A), Jerome, AZ 86331

Phone: (928) 634-5006 and toll free 1(800) 523-3554

Built in 1898 by David Connor, this twenty-room hotel offered a lavish stay to weary travelers and other visitors. The first floor had a saloon, card rooms, and billiards, while the second floor was where the bedrooms were located. The hotel had a run of bad luck burning down not once, but twice. It was rebuilt each time and renovated to its original grandeur. Like many of the other places in Jerome, the Connor Hotel was hit hard when the mines shut down. It stayed open, but was never as extravagant as it once was. By the 2000s, the hotel was renovated and opened once again. This is one of the many hotels in Jerome where ghost sightings have been reported.

Sign for the Connor Hotel, Jerome, 2011.

There several other hotels or bed and breakfast places to reside while in Jerome. This wonderful hillside town offers several choices of restaurants for your dining pleasure and a variety of shops to wander through. For information on Jerome's tourism, contact the following places:

Jerome Historical Society

Tourism website: www.azjerome.com

Address: 407 Clark Street, Jerome, AZ 86331

Phone: (928) 634-1066

Connor Hotel, Jerome, 2011.

Jerome Chamber of Commerce

Website: www.jeromechamber.com

Phone: (928) 634-2900

TOMBSTONE
(THE TOWN TOO TOUGH TO DIE)

Allen Street (main street), Tombstone, 2011.

If there was any town in the Arizona Territory that had a number of reported notorious events in the 1880s, it would be Tombstone. Like many of the other mining towns, Tombstone was founded after a rich vein of minerals was discovered by a prospector. This particular miner was named Edward Lawrence Schieffelin, who arrived in the San Pedro Valley in the summer of 1877. He lived at Camp Huachua (*wa-chu-ka*) scouting for Apache while searching the Mule Mountains on his days off and hoping to strike it rich. He was often asked what he was doing up in "them there mountains" and he would reply by simply saying, "to collect rocks." One soldier told him, "If you keep fooling around amongst the Apaches, the only rock you will find will be your tombstone." Finally, his persistence paid off when he discovered a large vein of silver near the area known as "Goose Flats." He named his claim "Tombstone," and, by early 1879, the City of Tombstone was built. The lots along the main street, or Allen Street, sold for $5 each. The entire town had 40 cabins and a population of 100 residents.

By 1880, there were four towns in the mining district that were thriving and Tombstone was the largest. The population exploded to 3,000, and a year later, it more than doubled to 7,000 people. Before the decade

O.K. Corral, Tombstone, 2011.

Schieffelin Hall, Tombstone, 2011.

Tombstone Courthouse, Tombstone, 2011.

was over, the number of men, women, and children was over 10,000. Tombstone had more brothels, gambling houses, and saloons than any other town in the Southwest. The town's Bird Cage Theatre was called, "The wildest, roughest, wickedest honky-tonk between Basin Street and the Barbary Coast" by the *New York Times*. The other theater in the desert settlement was named Schieffelin Hall, after the town's founder, Ed Schieffelin.

Many famous people walked the dusty streets of Tombstone. There were lawmen, outlaws, and celebrities, such as the Earps, Doc Holliday, Big Nose Kate, the Clantons, and Johnny Ringo, to name a few. (I write about six outlaws and their lives in chapter 3.) One of the most famous historical events taking place in Tombstone involved some of those well-known people. On October 26, 1881, the Gunfight at the O.K. Corral went down in a

Bird Cage Theatre, Tombstone, 2011.

bloody bath of riddled bullets, killing three and wounding others. Several vengeful acts followed this event, leaving lots of dead bodies throughout the town and surrounding area. During this time, the town's undertaker was busy taking bodies to the nearby cemetery, Boothill Graveyard, to be buried.

Tombstone continued to prosper for many years to come. The population was at its peak and all the businesses in town were flourishing. The turn of the century was good for Tombstone, but it also brought several tragedies from which the town could not return. Two fires almost destroyed the town while the mines were

experiencing floods. The miners dug holes in the pits trying to reach the silver. The cavities reached the 520-foot level, hitting the water table and flooding the mines. They tried to pump out the water, but after a couple years, they shut it down because of high costs. The high waters ruined several of the structures in town, causing the businesses to shut down. Many of the residents and visitors left the settlement and Tombstone became a virtual ghost town. By the early 1930s, approximately 150 people were living in the small desert city.

With a popular interest in history, people wanting a Wild West experience, and the many ghost sightings, Tombstone is thriving once again. Today, roughly 1,500 people are living in town, maintaining the past and legacy of this historic place. With all the prosperity and liveliness the present-day Tombstone is enjoying, it has earned the title, "The town too tough to die."

Tombstone has many attractions to make your Wild West experience more fun. Allen Street (Main Street) is blocked off to vehicles so that the horses and wagons can roam free. Take a stagecoach ride around town and see where many of the historic sites are located. Learn the history of each place and what famous person once walked the wooden floors and dirty streets. Tombstone has museums located in various places around town, such as the Courthouse and Bird Cage Theatre. There are plenty of places to eat and shop while watching an old west gunfight in the middle of the street. Tour the infamous O.K. Corral and stand where Wyatt Earp once stood. Along Main Street is the Ghost and Legends Tour with a ghostly Doc Holliday guiding you though the historic events that occurred in Tombstone. Finally, don't forget to stop and take an old-fashioned picture of yourself with your friends and family.

Old Time Photos on Main Street, Sharon and Julie, Tombstone, 2011.

VISITOR INFORMATION

Information and Tourist Guide

www.tombstoneweb.com

Tombstone Chamber of Commerce

www.tombstonechamber.com

City of Tombstone

www.cityoftombstone.com

Tombstone has all you need to make your Wild West experience complete. For those of you who would like to experience a ghost hunt, the Bird Cage Theatre can be rented for just that occasion. Contact them at (520) 457-3421 or www.tombstonebirdcage.com for prices and to book a time/date for your ghost hunt.

Directions: from Tucson, take U.S. Interstate 10, east to exit 303, merge onto AZ Highway 80 east to downtown Tombstone.

FAIRBANK
(HISTORIC TOWN SITE)

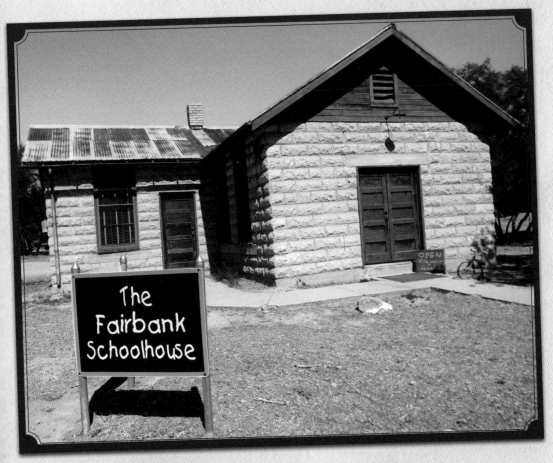

Fairbank Schoolhouse Museum and Visitor Center,
Fairbank, 2011.

If you decide to visit Tombstone, I would recommend you also go to see the historic site of Fairbank. This notable town is only 10 miles west of Tombstone on SR 82 east. It was built in 1881 on the old San Juan de las Boquillas y Nogales Mexican land grant and named after Nathanial Kellogg Fairbank. Fairbank was a businessman who put up his money to build the first railroad in the region. The first structure to be constructed in town was the Mercantile building in 1882. It was owned and operated by several families throughout the years while it was in service. By 1881, a railroad line was built between Fairbank and Bisbee and then extended to Douglas in 1901. A year later, the town was enjoying the bustling community with five saloons, a meat market, general store, three restaurants, a hotel, a Wells Fargo office, livery stables, post office, and many houses where the hundreds of residents dwelled.

By 1901, the settlement became mostly a family community and largely known for its

Inside the Fairbank Schoolhouse, Museum, and
Visitor Center, Fairbank, 2011.

abundance of trades. It had the reputation for being a much tamer place to live, unlike the unruly western towns that surrounded it. By the late 1920s, to accommodate the many children who lived in town, a schoolhouse was built. It was originally constructed as a one-room wood building, but when it burnt down, it was replaced by a block structure and two more rooms were added. Fairbank also had a large Chinese immigrant population who grew vegetables for the citizens of the town and the surrounding communities.

Fairbank survived a major earthquake in 1887 and continued thriving during the turn of the century when Tombstone's mines flooded. It remained the place where transportation was still the focal point for the Southwest until the price of copper dropped. In the Grand Central Mill, near Fairbank, they used the practice of mixing mercury to bind the silver and crushed ore. Many of the men suffered from the constant inhaling of the poisonous toxins and died young. In 1944, when the traffic from the railroads and mines diminished, the town closed the school. By the 1960s, the Southern Pacific Railroad ceased to run through the Fairbank Station. Seven years later, the Depot was removed and shortly afterwards, the last of the Fairbank residents left town for good. In 2008, the remaining railroad tracks were abandoned and removed.

Today, the schoolhouse can be seen just beyond the parking lot. Inside the building is a museum and recreation of the

Historic house, Fairbank, 2011.

classroom chronicling the early years of the tiny schoolhouse. Rows of students' chairs/desks are arranged in one of the rooms, along with a desk where the teacher once sat. The museum has displays of items once used by pioneers of the past who at one time walked the dusty streets of Fairbank.

After wandering through the town's history in the old schoolhouse, take a self-guided tour through the rest of the town. One of the first buildings to see is the Mercantile building. This place once housed a saloon, store, and post office. It was the first building constructed in town and stands as a testament to how durable structures were made. Even though the building is intact, time has taken its toll on it. Various repairs have been made

to keep it from further damage, both from animals and the weather.

Also on the tour, notice a couple of small wooden houses, a stable, outhouses, the railroads, and the Grand Central Mill. The historic buildings are surrounded by a grassy park with picnic tables. There are plenty of shady trees and benches to relax and take in the view.

A half-mile hike on a small trail will lead you to a hill where the town's cemetery sits. This cemetery has all but disappeared with only three visible graves with names on their headstones.

Historic building, Fairbank, 2011.

Front door of Fairbank Schoolhouse, 2011.

VISITOR INFORMATION

The Fairbank Schoolhouse and Fairbank Historic Townsite

Email: schoolhouse@sanpedroriver.org

Address: Highway 82, east of the San Pedro River, Fairbanks, AZ

Phone: (520) 457-3062

Open: Friday, Saturday, Sunday; 9:30 a.m. to 4:30 p.m.

Directions: from Tucson on Interstate 10, head south on Highway 90 and go about 18.5 miles to SR 82. Turn left (east) and travel about 10 miles to the entrance on the left (north) side of the road.

CHAPTER 3
Ascent of the Outlaws

The gallows at the Tombstone Courthouse,
Tombstone, 2011.

If you have ever wanted to walk the streets and stand in the place where a famous outlaw once stood, I take you there in this chapter. These outlaws left their marks in history and were present at some of Arizona's most famous events. They were seduced by the riches of the mining towns: hanging their hats and calling these places home. The towns offered many saloons and brothels to wet their hungry appetites. The battles between the lawmen and outlaws became as famous as the people themselves. Many of the known and lesser-known outlaws enjoyed terrorizing the innocent and weaker people. They were eventually caught and dealt with. Most of them ended up dead and buried somewhere in the Arizona desert. The legacies of these outlaws are certainly worth exploring.

THE CLANTONS

Their names were Fin, Ike, and Billy, and they were the more recognized of the Clanton children. Their father was Newman Haynes Clanton and was acknowledged by all as "Old Man Clanton." Their mother was Mariah Sexton Kelso and, together, she and Newman had seven children: five boys and two girls. Ike's and Billy's names will be forever connected with the historic gunfight at the O.K. Corral in Tombstone. Most of what is written in the history books or portrayed in movies refer to the brothers as outlaws, but there were many who considered them friends.

Fin (or Phin) was born Phineas Fay Clanton in December of 1845 in Callaway County, Missouri. He was the second Clanton boy behind first-born, John Wesley. His family moved many times when he was a child. In 1866, his mother died on the way to California. In 1877, he moved to Arizona to the Clanton Ranch and raised cattle with his father and brothers. Fin spent several years being accused of cattle rustling and stealing with his brother, Ike. He spent a little time in prison and was pardoned by the governor. In late 1882, he moved to Globe, Arizona, and raised Angora goats with his friend, Pete Spence. A year later,

Site of the famous gunfight at the O.K. Corral, Tombstone, 2011.

Globe Cemetery, Globe, 2010.

Fin and his brother-in-law, Ebin Stanley, were arrested and charged with cattle rustling. They were both found not guilty. In 1887, he was present with his brother, Ike, in Springerville, Arizona, when Ike was shot and killed trying to escape the lawmen who were looking for the brothers.

Fin lived a rather quiet life afterwards, working with his cattle business. On October 15, 1902, he married his love, Laura Jane Bound (or Neal). Four years later, on January 5, 1906, Fin died from pneumonia after a wagon accident left him out in the cold for a long period of time. Fin's grave can be found at the Globe Cemetery in Gila County, Globe, Arizona.

Fin's younger brother, Ike, had the wildest reputation of the whole Clanton bunch. He was born Joseph Isaac Clanton on June 1, 1847, and was nicknamed "Ike" by all. He was the third son of Old Man Clanton and Mariah. Throughout his adult life, he earned

a bad reputation as a nasty drunk, who loved both shooting off his mouth and pistols. Some folks said he loved his liquor, but too much booze often got him into many conflicts with the Earps and Doc Holliday. Ike was present at the Gunfight at the O.K. Corral on October 26, 1881, but he escaped unharmed. After that event, he and several others were accused of killing Morgan Earp and attempting to kill Virgil Earp. They were put on the Earp Vendetta Ride's revenge list. (This was a list of outlaw cowboys, led by U.S. Marshall Wyatt Earp, of men he felt were responsible for wounding his brother, Virgil, and killing his brother, Morgan. The Earp Vendetta Ride lasted from March 20 to April 15, 1802.) It was on June 1, 1887 when the law finally caught up with him. He, along with his brother, Fin, were held up on a cattle ranch in Springerville, Arizona, when the lawmen surrounded the place. While Fin gave up quietly, Ike decided

Boothill Graveyard, Tombstone, 1995.

to escape. He was shot twice by Jonas V. Brighton, with the fatal blow passing through his heart. Ike fell off his horse and hit the ground, dead.

Until 1996, it remained a mystery where he was buried. A relative and grave expert found his shallow grave under a large tree near Eagle Creek in Greenlee County, Arizona. His bones remain there to this very day.

The youngest of the Clanton boys was Billy. He was born William Harrison Clanton in 1862 in Hamilton County, Texas. In 1877, the Clanton Ranch was up and running and Billy helped his father operate it. Many of the town's folks liked Billy and saw him as a hard worker.

Black Mariah hearse, Bird Cage Theatre, Tombstone, 2011.

However, the Earps accused him, his father, and brother, Ike, of being horse thieves.

Billy was only 19 when his father was ambushed and killed in New Mexico. On August 1, 1881, Old Man Clanton was riding in Guadalupe Canyon in Animas Valley with other men. They were surprised by a group of Mexicans and attacked. At the end, many of the men were killed along with Clanton. Later that same year, Billy would lose his life to a fierce gunfight. It was October 26, 1881, when the Earps and Doc Holliday walked down the dusty streets of Tombstone towards the O.K. Corral. A gunfight ensued and when the dust settled, Billy, along with Frank and Tom McLaury, laid dead in the bloodstained dirt. Billy's life was cut down at the age of 19.

Their funeral was one of the largest in Tombstone's history with all being buried at the Boothill Graveyard. It was also told that Ike and Fin had their father's remains moved next to Billy's a year after his death.

This article was written in the *Tombstone Nugget* newspaper on October 28, 1881:

AN IMPOSING FUNERAL
The burial of the Dead Cowboys—An Immense Procession, Etc.

While it was not entirely expected, the funeral of Billy Clanton and Thomas and Frank McLaury, yesterday, was the largest ever witnessed in Tombstone. It was advertised to take place at 3 o'clock, but it was about 4 o'clock before the cortege moved, yet a large number had gathered at the undertaker's long before the first time mentioned. The bodies of the three men, neatly and tastefully dressed, were

Skeleton cowboys playing cards at entrance of Ghosts and Legends Tour, Tombstone, 2011.

placed in handsome caskets with heavy silver trimmings. Upon each was a silver plate bearing the name, age, birthplace and date of the death of each. A short time before the funeral, photographs were taken of the dead. The procession was headed by the Tombstone brass band playing the solemn and touching march of the dead. The first wagon contained the body of Billy Clanton, followed by those of THE MCLAURY BOYS. A few carriages came next in which were friends and relatives of the deceased, among whom were Ike and Fin Clanton. After these were about three hundred persons on foot, twenty-two carriages and buggies and one four horse stage, and the horsemen, making a line nearly two blocks in length. The two brothers were buried in one grave and the young Clanton close by those who were his friends in life and companions in death. The inscription upon the plates of the caskets stated that Thomas McLaury was 25 years of age, Frank McLaury 29 years of age, both natives of Mississippi, and that William H. Clanton was 19 years of age and a native of Texas. "Yet a little sleep, a little slumber, a little folding of the hands to sleep."

Visitors have the opportunity to walk in the footsteps of the infamous Clanton brothers. Stop at the O.K. Corral in Tombstone, Arizona, and see where Billy was standing when he was gunned down. Also visit Boothill Graveyard and see where Billy, the McLaury brothers, and Old Man Clanton's last resting places are located. While walking along Allen Street of Tombstone, enjoy the Ghost and Legends Tour. This self-guided tour is located where the Wells Fargo Company once stood; also a saloon, barber, and cigar shop. Now it is a walk-through attraction where Tombstone's history comes alive.

VISITOR INFORMATION

O.K. Corral

Website: www.ok-corral.com

Address: P.O. Box 367, Tombstone, AZ 85638

Phone: (520) 457-34565

Hours: open every day from 9 a.m. to 5 p.m..

Boothill Graveyard

Website: www.boothillgraves.com

Address: 408 N. Highway 80, Tombstone, AZ 85638

Phone: (520) 457-3300

Hours: 7:30 a.m. to dusk

Ghost and Legends Tour

Website: www.tombstonechamber. com/Ghosts-and-Legends

Address:
414 Allen Street, Tombstone, AZ 85638

Phone: (520) 457-3045

Hours: 9 a.m. to 5 p.m.

* You can also travel to the Globe Cemetery in Globe and see where Phineas Clanton was buried. See Chapter 2 for information on the City of Globe.

Globe Cemetery

Globe, Gila County, Arizona

Websites: www.Arizonagravestones. org/cemetery.php and www. findagrave.com

E. L. FERGUSON
(PETE SPENCE)

Drawing of Pete Spence in prison clothes by Julie Ferguson.

What first grabbed my attention about E. L. Ferguson was that we shared the same last name. I noticed it on his headstone while visiting the Globe Cemetery and took a picture of it. When I looked him up on my computer, I couldn't find much information on the man as E. L. Ferguson, but there were lots of interesting stories written about his alias, Pete Spence. His life was as intriguing as other notorious outlaws even though he wasn't as well known. He also rubbed elbows and rode along with many famous people of the Wild West era.

He was born Elliot Larkin Ferguson, in 1851, in the state of Louisiana. During his notorious robbing and murderous days, he went under the alias, Pete Spence. Not much was told of his early life, parents, or whether he had siblings. It wasn't until June 29, 1874, when he enlisted in the Frontier Company of Texas Rangers and served under Captain Warren Wallace that any record of his existence became known. His rank was second lieutenant and he was known to have a bit of a temper. While serving, he shot a man, inflicting a flesh wound. Luckily, the man survived, but Ferguson disappeared shortly afterwards and left the Rangers. His name reappeared in 1878 when he committed a robbery and was running from the law. His journey took him to the Arizona Territory and he decided to hang his hat in Tombstone. It was there that he changed his name to Peter M. Spence and lived in a small house across from the Earp home. He struck up a friendship with the Clanton family and became business partners with Frank Stilwell. After Morgan Earp was shot and killed in 1882, many pointed their fingers at Spence as the murderer. It was never proven and, shortly afterwards, he left Arizona, but only for a brief time.

Stories circulated throughout the West that Spence killed at least four men. He was convicted and sentenced to prison for the murder of Rodney O'Hara. In a fit of anger, Spence pistol-whipped O'Hara to death. He was sentenced to five years in the Yuma Arizona Territorial Prison beginning on June 10, 1893.

He listed his occupation as "teamster" and nearest relative as Mollie E. Spence of Los

also in charge of burro trains, which brought supplies to the Globe area. His friend, Fin, died in 1906 and four years later, on April 2, 1910, he married Fin's widow, Laura, and used his birth name of E. L. Ferguson.

The following article was written in the *Globe Daily Arizona Silver Belt* the next day, Sunday, April 3, 1910.

LENGTHY ROMANCE

After an acquaintanceship of many years, Mrs. F. Clanton and E. L. Ferguson, better known to his many friends as Pete Spence, were married at Webster Springs Ranch yesterday, by Judge Hinton Thomas. Both the bride and groom have lived in this part of the territory for many years, Ferguson having come to Globe in 1875. For some time, however, he has lived in Mexico, meeting Mrs. Ferguson on his return and reviving an old friendship which soon united the couple at the Hymeneal altar.

E. L. Ferguson's headstone, Globe Cemetery, 2010.

I do question when Spence actually arrived in Globe. The article says he moved there in 1875, but he was released from prison in 1893. I don't have any information stating if he lived in Globe previous to his time in prison, but the man is a puzzling conundrum.

Spence died in 1914, but it is unknown as to the exact location of his grave. The original wood indicator bearing his name and marking the place of his burial has been demolished. Although some say he is buried next to Fin Clanton in the Globe Cemetery, I found his headstone located in a nearby site.

To walk in Pete Spence's footsteps, you should visit Tombstone and Globe. Both towns are mentioned in Chapter 2. I give you detailed history and information on all the places to see while in each place. E. L. Ferguson's grave can be found in the Globe Cemetery. For more information, check out this website: www. findagrave.com.

Angeles, California. There are questions as to whether this information is correct because in the U.S. Census, taken in June of 1885, it lists his wife as Josefina Spence, age 24. Others question whether he was married at all. The mystery that is Pete Spence is still unfolding even today.

Even though Spence killed a man, he only served eighteen months in prison and moved to Globe after being released. He and his longtime friend, Fin Clanton, owned a goat ranch in the Galiuro Mountains. Spence was

CURLY BILL BROCIUS

Drawing by Julie Ferguson.

As a part of the Tombstone Cowboys, Curly Bill earned a reputation as the fastest shot of the entire bunch of hooligans. It was told that he could shoot a running jackrabbit, candle flames without touching the candles, and quarters between the fingers of anyone who was crazy enough to offer their assistance. He was also known as a nasty drunk who enjoyed making people dance by shooting his gun at their feet. Sometimes when he was feeling particularly unruly, he would have them strip naked first. Throughout his life he was known for pulling off several different exploits. He once held his pistol on a Reverend and wanted him to perform a service for him and his group of cowboys. He was also caught padding a ballot box in San Simon because he didn't want Bob Paul to win as sheriff. Curly Bill's boisterous acts also consisted of ambushing a mule train and taking all the silver aboard.

It was while he was in Tombstone he became known as "Arizona's Most Famous Outlaw." In 1880, and sometime around midnight one night, Curly Bill was wandering the streets drunk and being very offensive. When Marshal Fred White attempted to arrest him, his gun went off and he wounded himself. Curly Bill claimed it was an accident and White concurred just before he died two days after the incident. People reported seeing Wyatt Earp pistol-whipping Bill just before throwing him in jail. Curly spent a couple of months in jail until he was acquitted with a ruling of accidental death.

Things were not easy for the known outlaw after spending time incarcerated. After an attempt on Virgil Earp's life, he was one of the men accused of pulling off the shooting.

The Wild West had many fascinating people written into the history books. In the late 19th century, a band of outlaws formed a group called "The Cowboys." This collection of men was made up of cattle rustlers and thieves found in the southern part of the Arizona Territory. One of their members made his mark in the American Old West history as a fast gunman and criminal. His name was William "Curly Bill" Brocius and he was born in 1845 in Crawfordsville, Indiana. He was described as a tall, stocky man with freckles and dark, curly hair.

Sign of Cochise County Sheriff's Office, Tombstone County Courthouse, 2011.

Grave at Fairbank Cemetery, Fairbank, 2011.

Without solid proof, he was put on the Earp Vendetta Ride's revenge list and was being hunted down along with others. On March 24, 1882, Wyatt Earp snuck up on Bill's camp near Iron Springs and killed him with one or two shotgun blasts to the chest from about fifty feet away. Some say he was able to get a shot off at Wyatt before dying, but only winged his coat. The exact location of his final resting spot has been rumored to be along the Babocomari River near the McLaury ranch, and five miles west of the historic town of Fairbank, Arizona. His gravesite is lost by all the vegetation that has grown around that area over time.

To see where Curly Bill shot Marshal Fred White, visit Tombstone. Check Chapter 2 for the history of Tombstone and other places around town to see. In the Bird Cage Theatre's museum is the barber chair Curly Bill sat in whenever he got a shave and a haircut.

Barber chair used many times by Curly Bill, Tombstone, 2011.

VISITOR INFORMATION

Bird Cage Theatre

Website: www.tombstonebirdcage.com

Address: 535 E. Allen Street, Tombstone, AZ 85638

Phone: (520) 457-3421

For information on the historic site of Fairbank, Arizona, check out Chapter 2.

BIG NOSE KATE

Sign over the Big Nose Kate's Saloon, Tombstone, 2011.

There were many stories written in the history books about the outlaw men of the Wild West. The men may have ruled much of the stories, but there are women who earned the right to be outlaws and were as famous as the men they loved. One such lady was Big Nose Kate. Her problematic relationship with Doc Holliday was infamous.

She came into this world as Mary Katherine Horony (or Haroney) on November 7, 1850, in Budapest, Hungary. Her father was a Hungarian physician and brought his family to the United States in 1862, after being appointed personal surgeon to Mexico's Emperor, Maximillian. After

the disintegration of Max's reign of power in 1865, the family made their home in Davenport, Iowa, in a largely German community.

When she was in her early teens, both her parents died within a month of each other, leaving Kate and her younger siblings to foster care. It was in 1867 that Kate became the ward of Otto Smith, but ran away from him shortly afterwards. She hid on a steamship bound for St. Louis, Missouri, and was able to stay aboard even after she was caught by the ship's captain. She took his last name and enrolled in a convent school as Kate Fisher. A few years later, she met a dentist named Silas Melvin

One of the rooms used by soiled doves, basement of the Bird Cage Theatre, Tombstone, 2011.

The San Jose House, Tombstone, 2011.

and married him. They had child together, but sadly Silas and the baby became ill and died the same year.

Kate took on various occupations in order to survive while moving from town to town. She ended up in Dodge City in 1874 and worked for Nellie Bessie Earp, wife of James Earp. She was a dance hall girl known as Kate Elder and entertained men on the side as a soiled dove (another name for a prostitute). After living there for awhile, in 1877 she decided to move to Fort Griffin, Texas. It was there where she was given the moniker "Big Nose Kate" because of her prominent nose. One evening, while in a saloon, she met a card

Big Nose Kate's headstone under her real name at the time of death, Mary K. Cummings, Prescott, 2011.

dealer named Doc Holliday. She knew of Doc's fierce temper, but this sassy and willful woman was not worried. Her rage was equally matched to his and she would not back down from an argument. The mischievous side of Kate was intrigued by Doc and she would do anything to protect her man. She proved this by aiding in his escape after a barroom scuffle left a man stabbed to death by Doc. Even though Doc claimed it was self-defense, the sheriff still attempted to arrest him. Kate stood at the doorway with a pistol in each hand while Doc made his escape with her following right behind him.

Kate and Doc made their way back to Dodge City and decided to make a life together. He promised to hang up his gambling hat and she would give up her life as a soiled dove. They lived in a boarding house as Mr. and Mrs. J. H. Holliday, but because of their tumultuous relationship, the duo separated countless times.

Years of a shattered and torn relationship was finally tested when Kate betrayed Doc, breaking their liaison for good. It was early 1881 when a drunk and angry Kate lied to authorities about Doc being part of a stagecoach robbery. Even though she recanted her statement, their association was over once and for all. Doc made his home in Tombstone, while Kate lived in Globe and ran a boarding house for miners. Later, Doc, who suffered with tuberculosis, ended up moving to Colorado and lived in a hotel/sanatorium. He died in bed on November 8, 1887, at the age of 36. There were reports of Kate spending time with him until his death.

In 1898, while still living in Colorado, Kate married a blacksmith, George M. Cummings. They moved back to Arizona, but only after a couple of years of matrimony, Kate divorced him. By 1900, she worked as a housekeeper for a man named Howard in Dos Cabezas, Arizona.

She stayed with him until his death in 1930. A year later, she wrote the Governor of Arizona asking to be permitted to live in the "Arizona Pioneers Home." Since she was not legally born in the United States, she was not eligible, so Kate lied and said she was born in Davenport, Iowa. They accepted her and she lived there until her death on November 2, 1940, just shy of her 90th birthday. She was buried under the name, Mary K. Cummings in the Arizona Pioneer Home Cemetery in Prescott, Arizona. The headstone on her grave simply has her name and the years of her birth and death.

Big Nose Kate lived in many places around the state of Arizona. She once lived in Globe where she ran a boarding house. (The history and places to see while in Globe are outlined in Chapter 2.) She once walked the streets of Tombstone. When you visit Tombstone, be sure to check out the saloon/restaurant that bears the name of this fascinating Wild West woman.

PRESCOTT

Whiskey Row, 2011, Prescott.

Prescott is one of my favorite places to visit in Arizona. It is a small city with lots of history. In 1864, Prescott became the capital of the Arizona Territory, but eventually it was moved to Phoenix in 1889. Many of the locals will tell you that it is pronounced *Pres-kit* and not *Pres-cott*.

One of Prescott's famous attractions is Whiskey Row. It houses the red-light district area with many saloons and hotels. The Palace Saloon was built in 1877 and was filled with the highest standard liqueur and decorated with the most elaborate furniture from all over the world. Big Nose Kate, Doc Holliday, and even the Earps were known to hang out at this sophisticated saloon. As grand as Whiskey Row's history was, it was met with many tragedies. In 1883, a fire obliterated most of Whiskey Row, destroying many of the buildings, including the original Palace Saloon. Even though the structure was rebuilt with stones and bricks, it burnt down again after another huge fire ravished downtown Prescott. In 2012, sadly, the historic Bird Cage Saloon and another attached business caught fire and burned to the ground. Both places are currently being restored and rebuilt to their former glory. Whiskey Row is definitely worth your time while you are visiting Prescott. It is located across from the historic Prescott Courthouse and park.

VISITOR INFORMATION

Yavapai County Courthouse

Address: 120 S. Cortez Street, Prescott, AZ, 86303

Phone: (928) 771-3300

Fax: (928) 771-3302

HOTEL VENDOME

Hotel Vendome, Prescott, 2011.

Prescott has many hotels and B&B's for you to lay your hat while visiting this wonderful city. One of the places where I enjoy staying is the Hotel Vendome. This place is rich in history and located near downtown Prescott. It is a two-story bed and breakfast with an old-world feel to it. It was originally a residential home, but now this red brick structure has sixteen rooms that are all decorated with an old-fashioned flare. The front is adorned with a huge porch and second-story veranda where you can sit outside and enjoy Prescott's amazing weather. For that ghost hunter in you, the hotel is said to be haunted by the ghost of Abby Byr and her cat, Noble.

VISITOR INFORMATION

Website: www.vendomehotel.com

Address: 230 S. Cortez Street, Prescott, AZ 86303

Phone: (928) 776-0900

Email: info@vendomehotel.com

Hours: 8 a.m. to 8 p.m. (Sunday to Thursday); 8 a.m. to 9 p.m. (Friday to Saturday)

* To find out more information and what to see and where to sleep and eat while in Prescott, check out these websites: www.cityofprescott.net and www.visit-prescott.com.

PEARL HART

Pearl's life is a bit of a mystery with little-known documents to back up the many stories. In 1871, Pearl Hart began life as Pearl Taylor in Lindsay, Ontario, Canada. Her father was a civil engineer and moved the family to Ohio in 1878, where later, at the age of 17, Pearl married Frank (Frederick or Brett) Hart. Frank was an alcoholic gambler with an ill temper who abused her on many occasions. Life wasn't always that bad while Frank had a job as a manager and bartender in a nearby hotel. During this time, they started to experiment with marijuana and other drugs. The drinking got out of hand as well. Eventually, Pearl got pregnant and had a baby girl. This was not what Frank wanted, so one night he repeatedly hit Pearl so hard, she hit the ground and was out cold. He left the both of them for parts unknown. Having no money or a place to go, she moved back to Canada, but soon left her daughter with her mother and moved back to Arizona. Even though Pearl hated the West, she survived by doing laundry for others and cooking at the local café.

In 1893, while Pearl was working in Phoenix, she ran into Frank once more. The

Drawing by Julie Ferguson.

Sometime in the late 1890s, while living in Arizona, Pearl heard that her mother was gravely ill and she needed to go home. Desperate for money, she hooked up with a no-good miner using a rumored alias, Joe Boot. Together, the two of them devised various schemes to get money. One of them involved Pearl flirting with men and enticing them to go back to her room. In the room, Boot would be waiting, knock the unsuspecting man out, and they would steal all his belongings. This was fine for awhile, but the pair got greedy and wanted more. On May 30, 1899, the two of them decided to rob the Globe-to-Florence stagecoach near the settlement of Troy and Kane Spring Canyon. Pearl cut her hair, dressed in man's clothing, and armed herself with a .38 revolver. Boot held a gun on the victims while Pearl stole two firearms and money. They got a total of $450 and took the driver's gun while fleeing south towards Benson. After getting lost, they were captured near the north side of Benson and charged with armed robbery.

While serving time in a Tucson jail, the petite, five-foot-tall woman earned the nickname, "Bandit Queen." She also felt affection for an inmate trustee named, Ed Hogan, who was a petty thief. Hogan aided in her escape on October 12, 1899, but she was recaptured two weeks later in New Mexico. While on the run, she became more infamous. After making the judge angry for her behavior, she was sent to the Yuma Territorial Prison to serve out her time. While incarcerated, she loved all the attention her notorious reputation brought her. She had fun posing for pictures with anyone who would ask. On December 19, 1902, she was pardoned by Governor Alexander Brodie and released. It was reported that she moved to Kansas and just seemed to vanish from existence.

Her later life is mysterious with one theory being that she owned a cigar shop in Kansas until her death in 1952. Another story has her living in San Francisco and also dying in 1952. Yet another claim has her living a private life with her husband of fifty years, George Calvin "Cal" Bywater, in Dripping Springs, Arizona. According

pair moved around to several places where Frank once worked in a sideshow and Pearl did odd jobs to keep them afloat. During this time, she became enamored with strong women figures, such as Annie Oakley and Julia Ward Howe, who was an activist and poet. These women inspired her to gain the power to leave Frank for a second time. After moving to Colorado, she found out she was pregnant yet again with Frank's baby. Like before, she moved back to Canada, had a son, and once again left him with her mother and moved to Phoenix. She quickly became very lonely, and suffered from depression. She tried to commit suicide a few times, but was stopped by her friends.

Stagecoach in Tombstone, 2011.

to her headstone, she died on December 28, 1955. Also, according to her headstone, she was born on November, 13, 1876 and not 1871. She is buried next to her husband in the Pinal Cemetery, which is located near Superior, Arizona. Although some details of her life are uncertain and often inconsistent, Pearl is acknowledged as the only known female stagecoach robber in Arizona's history, earning her the nicknames of "Bandit Queen" or "Lady Bandit."

Pearl Hart's headstone under her married name, "Bywater," Pinal Cemetery, Superior, 2010.

Like the infamous Big Nose Kate, Pearl traveled and lived in many places all over the Arizona Territory:

Apache Leap Mountain, 2010, Superior.

PHOENIX

This is the city where Pearl first lived when she moved to Arizona. She was married to alcoholic gambler, Frank. Her life with him was a living nightmare. Phoenix is the largest city and capital of Arizona. It was founded in 1861 and officially became a city in 1881. It is located in the center of the state, in Maricopa County, and in the northeastern area of the Sonoran Desert. To find out more of what Phoenix has to offer, check out this website: www. visitphoenix.com.

BENSON

This town is where Pearl and Joe Boot were captured after committing armed robbery of a stagecoach. Benson is located in Cochise County, Arizona, forty-five miles east-southeast of Tucson. It was founded in 1880 as a rail terminal for the area, and still serves as one today. For more information on Benson, visit www.cityofbenson.com.

TUCSON

Pearl served time in the Tucson jail, until she escaped in 1899. Tucson has many attractions and places to see. There are varied historic sites for you to enjoy while visiting this magnificent city. Tucson is often referred to as "The Old Pueblo." For Tucson's places to see, visit: www. visittucson.org.

YUMA TERRITORIAL PRISON

Pearl served out the rest of her prison sentence at this prison until she was released in 1902. This is also a great place to conduct a ghost hunt. Many claims of apparitions, disembodied voices, and strange noises have been report by many.

Yuma Territorial Prison State Historic Park

Website: http://azstateparks.com/Parks/YUTE/index.html

Address: 100 N. Prison Hill Road, Yuma, AZ 85364

Phone: (928) 783-4771

Park Hours: 9 a.m. to 5 p.m.

DRIPPING SPRINGS

This is where Pearl lived with her husband Calvin Bywater. For more information: www.usa.com/dripping-springs-az.htm

SUPERIOR

This town is located near the Pinal Cemetery where Pearl Hart rests in peace. Superior was hit hard with the slumping economy and the mines drying up. It is apparent when you drive through Superior's downtown and see all the abandoned buildings. For the urban explorer, this place is a gold mine for taking amazing photos. The eeriness of the town's empty places has attracted Hollywood. The location has been used in such movies as *U Turn*, *Eight Legged Freaks*, *The Prophecy*, *Skinwalkers*, and *The Gauntlet* for example. Take time to visit this small town and see what it has to offer: www.superior-arizona.com

Don't forget to visit Pearl Hart's grave:

Pinal Cemetery
Website: www.findagrave.com
Address: Gila County, AZ

For other information regarding Pearl, visit: www.legendsofamerica.com/we-pearlhart.html

---

GOLD DOLLAR

Display of "Soiled Doves" property in Bird Cage Theatre, Tombstone 2011.

There are many tales about the remarkable people who once walked the dusty streets of Tombstone. One such story is that of a Crystal Palace dancer and murderer named Gold Dollar. She was first known to town's folks as Little Gertie, but with her long golden hair, fair complexion, and earning a gold dollar as payment for service bestowed, she was given the nickname of "Gold Dollar." She was tiny in stature, feisty, and very protective of her man, Billy Milgreen, a local gambler. The petite prostitute threatened bodily harm to any woman of Tombstone who flirted with her man. Most were afraid of her, except one.

Trouble came to town in the name of Margarita, an attractive Mexican woman

Basement of Bird Cage Theatre, Tombstone, 2011.

who worked as a soiled dove at the Bird Cage Theatre. With her creamy bronze skin, this mysterious woman with long black hair immediately set her dark eyes on Billy. Many of the men were mesmerized by her beauty, and Billy was no exception. Margarita was aware of Gold Dollar's temper and her threats, but it didn't stop her allured behavior towards the stimulating gambler. Gold Dollar got wind of her flirtations and marched over to the Bird Cage Theatre. She threatened to cut out Margarita's heart if the behavior did not end. Margarita was not intimidated by Gold Dollar and wouldn't back off under pressure.

Billy promised Gold Dollar he would not let Margarita's aggressive flirting get to him if she would let him gamble. She trusted her man

and let him head off to the Bird Cage for a high-stakes poker game. Margarita was determined to grab his attention by swaggering gracefully across the floor, strutting around the table, and then finally dropping in his lap overwhelming him with kisses. Gold Dollar went to the Bird Cage to check up on Billy and saw Margarita sitting in his lap. She grabbed a fist full of hair, and pulled her off. Gold Dollar stabbed Margarita with a four-inch, double-edged stiletto and either plunged it in her side or in her chest and almost cut her heart out. Either way, Margarita died of her wounds in a pool of blood. The Sheriff was called and Gold Dollar ran out of the Bird Cage with the bloody stiletto in hand. She hid the small dagger behind the building and since the weapon was never

Bird Cage Theatre, Tombstone, 2011.

found, murder charges were never filed against her. She ended up quietly leaving town, and was followed by Billy months later. It was over 100 years later that the stiletto was found, and was discovered behind the Bird Cage Theatre.

THE BIRD CAGE THEATRE

When walking down Allen Street to the end of town, you will find the Bird Cage Theatre. It is a brick building with three sets of double doors in the front, each having a half-moon window above. Once inside, there is a feeling of stepping back in time. To the right are narrow stairs leading to the catwalk and upper loft where the soiled doves enticed the cowboys and miners to come up. On the ceiling above, bullet holes are still visible, reminding us of

the theatre's violent history. To the left is the display case to pay for the self-guided tour, then on through a door to the Bird Cage's bygone days.

The theatre is a museum of original items found inside the building by the owners. Along the walls are several display cabinets with many dusty artifacts: some are Wild West pieces used and worn by the people who passed through Tombstone. Other things along the walls are pieces of antique furniture and pianos. Hanging on the walls are many photos of the famous and not-so-famous people who once lived in Tombstone. In back of the main room is the stage and a set of wooden stairs leading to the back room. Above the main floor are the rooms or

Main floor of Bird Cage Theatre, Tombstone, 2011.

cages with creepy mannequins hanging out in some of them. In the center of the room are more antiques, desks, poker tables, sewing machines, craps tables, and artifacts.

To your left, when climbing the wood stairs to the back room, is the Russian room behind glass. To the left in the back room is a wall dedicated to the soiled doves who once worked there. Some of their items and an old tub can be found in the back display case. Next to that is where the Black Mariah hearse sits. This creepy vehicle once carried the bodies of those killed in Tombstone to the Boothill Graveyard.

To the right are the stairs leading to the basement and poker room. This space has a display case, a bar, two prostitute's rooms, and a couple of poker tables set up as if the cowboys were still playing. Enter through a set of doors into the gift shop. From there, exit the Bird Cage Theatre.

VISITOR INFORMATION

Websites: www.arizona-leisure.com/bird-cage-theatre.html and www.tombstonebirdcage.com

Address: 535 E. Allen Street, Tombstone, AZ 85638

Phone: 1(800) 457-3423 or (520) 457-3421

Hours: 8 a.m. to 6 p.m., daily; price: $10 each

Ghost tours – adults only (18 and over with proof of age) $20 each; 9:30 p.m. ghost hunts – private hunts with a group ($100 an hour); after ghost tours

Crystal Palace, Tombstone, 2011.

Gold Dollar danced at the Crystal Palace Saloon in its Wild West days. The building was constructed in 1879 and was first called the Golden Eagle Brewery. Located on the corner of 5th and Allen Street, the historic building was later known as the Crystal Palace. The Crystal Palace Saloon now provides a wonderful meal, tasty drinks, and the Old West atmosphere.

VISITOR INFORMATION

Website:
www.crystalpalacesaloon.com

Address: 436 E. Allen Street, Tombstone, AZ 85638

Phone: (520) 457-3611

CHAPTER 4

Forsaken to the Elements

AUTHOR NOTE

Always obtain permission before entering any private property. Follow directions for any posted signs. Trespassing is illegal and can land you in jail!

Research the following locations to receive your own appointments or permissions before visiting.

This chapter concentrates on the urban explorer and photographer enthusiast. There are many unknown places throughout the state of Arizona that once enjoyed the bustling excitement of life. Some of these places are homes or apartments where families once lived and raised their children. The one-time busy hotels once existed for people to rest their weary bones and stood as places to stop while on business trips or vacations. Yet other places were businesses and factories, which people depended on for their livelihood and survival.

Kelvin, Arizona, 2013.

Today, these locations sit abandoned because of the distressful economy and because the people living or working in each locality have moved on. The cruel Arizona desert weather has taken its toll on all the places I acknowledge in this chapter. Some of the forsaken buildings I have visited have all but disappeared, along with entire towns. The ones I show here can still be traveled to and explored as they continue to stand as empty reminders of times past.

DISCARDED MOTEL

Abandoned motel, Gila Bend, 2010.

Sitting along Interstate 8, off Arizona State Route 85, near the city of Gila Bend is an abandoned adobe motel. Driving up and parking in the dirt lot, explorers will notice all the many rooms without doors, windows, or ceilings and wonder what this place may have been like in its heyday. Who laid their hats and rested their tired bones on the comfy beds here while on vacation or perhaps a business trip? We may never know what stories this place could tell.

Inside motel, Gila Bend, 2010.

Today, this property is an empty shell with a broken TV sitting out front, imparting a feeling for the essence of the place. The walls are chipping and the "M" in the word "motel" is barely visible. Sitting outside the rooms are items that were once part of the decor. Inside, some of the rooms are missing walls while the remaining ones have broken drywall and chipping paint. The ceiling is open in most of the rooms where the sky is apparent. One room had a dirty pillow on the floor; another had a bar suspended from the ceiling with a couple of rusty hangers still drooping from it. In the end room sits a fireplace amongst a pile of junk. The stones are still reflecting the bright colors of each rock from which the fireplace was made. Found in the corner of each room is the tiny bathroom. Some still have the toilets, although most are broken and there are torn shower curtains hanging in some of the rooms. If you decide to visit to go urban exploring, be aware of the summertime critters and sharp items scattered on the floors in each room.

Empty hangers inside motel, Gila Bend, 2010.

Space Age Restaurant, Gila Bend, 2010.

Sign for Space Age Lodge, Gila Bend, 2013.

Gila Bend has many more sites for you to visit while urban exploring. There are countless abandoned buildings around town along with quirky shops and restaurants.

Along the main road is where the Space Age Restaurant is located. I have been there a couple of times on my travels through town. Their Bacon Cheeseburgers are amazing and one of the tastiest burgers I have ever had. Next to the restaurant is the Space Age Lodge (Best Western), where you can stay if you decide to spend the night in Gila Bend. Behind the restaurant is an old wood water tower that reminds me of the 1960s television show, *Petticoat Junction*.

VISITOR INFORMATION

Space Age Restaurant (UFO Café)

Address: 401 E. Pima Street,
Gila Bend, AZ 85337

Phone: (928) 683-2761

Space Age Lodge (Best Western)

Address: 401 E. Pima Street,
Gila Bend, AZ 85337

Phone: (928) 683-2273

Check in: 2 p.m.; check out: 12 p.m.

If you want to shop at an unusual antique and rusty metal art store while in Gila Bend, check out the Cactus N Stuff shop. This place has a great variety of antiques, Arizona items, and hand-made metal western art.

Front of Cactus N Stuff shop, Gila Bend, 2013.

Cactus N Stuff

Website: www.cactusnstuff.com

Address: 404 W. Pima Street,
Gila Bend, AZ 85337

Phone: (928) 683-2411

Email: gilabendcactusnstuff@earthlink.net

There are other places to stay while visiting Gila Bend. One is the historic Stout's Hotel along the main drag of Pima Street (Hwy 85). To find out more information on the town of Gila Bend, check out the following:

Gila Bend Chamber of Commerce

Websites: www.gilabendaz.org and
www.gilabendazchamber.com

Stout's Hotel, Gila Bend, 2013.

Address: P.O. Box CC, Gila Bend, AZ 85337

Phone: (928) 420-1964

Email: info@gilabendazchamber.com

Gila Bend sign, 2013.

THE BEE APARTMENTS

Miami, 2010

The first time my friend and I stumbled across this gem was while hunting for abandoned places in Miami, Arizona, during December of 2010. Just above the downtown area of this mining settlement and off Interstate 60, sits several amazing abandoned structures. After enjoying a tasty Mexican lunch, we decided to walk towards the center of town and check out the antique shops. We noticed the many concrete stairs, which started on the main drag and seemed to endlessly make their way up to the houses above. We were happy to see there were dirt roads leading to those homes and we wanted to explore them.

While walking down the dusty street in downtown Miami and taking pictures of all the abandoned structures, we spotted an interesting house. We were looking at the rear of the place and it appeared to be a small, single-family home. It had a worn-out and rusty "For Sale" sign near the back entrance with the name of the realtor on it. We wanted to get a better look at the place and drove down to check out the front. To our surprise, the place was much bigger than we'd expected. It was two stories with several doors leaving us with the conclusion that it must have been an apartment complex at one time. A neighbor caught us snooping around and confirmed it used to be apartments. He also told us that the place has sat empty for more than fifteen years.

From the front, the two-car garage can be seen with no doors and old, rusty items inside. One portion of the building was unpainted with rotting wood planks and a huge tree in front. This looked like it may have been some type of a storage room. The other section of the building, where several rooms were located, was painted blue, but was now chipping away with time. As we climbed the cement stairs to get a closer look at the inside, we were stopped by the buzzing of thousands of bees. Inside the porch's decaying ceiling boards was an enormous beehive that looked to be about four feet in diameter. We stood still and decided not to pursue any further. If they were "killer" bees, we knew they would chase us all the way home without breaking a sweat. Because of the many bees, we decided to name the place, "The Bee Apartments." Be cautious of this place; not only are the bees a danger, but it is private property.

Back of abandoned apartments, Miami, 2010.

The second time we drove through Miami was in July of 2011. We were on our way to Globe to conduct a ghost hunt at the old jail and decided to stop. We found our Bee Apartments, but they looked so much different. The first time we saw this incredible place was in the winter when all the shrubbery and trees surrounding the lot were baron. This time it was summer and the place was almost invisible with the abundant growth of the trees and bushes. Of course, we had to climb the cement steps to see if the bees were still

Front of abandoned apartments, Miami, 2010.

present. Not only were they still buzzing around the porch, but there appeared to be more of them. We also noticed that the hive was larger and still tucked under the porches ceiling boards. I can't imagine what will happen if the hive gets much larger. It just may hit the ground after the rotting boards holding it up finally break from all the weight. The next time we find ourselves in Miami, we will stop at the abandoned apartments and see if the bees are still living there.

Front rooms and porch of abandoned apartments, Miami, 2010.

Abandoned "Bee Apartments",
Miami, 2010.

The mining town of Miami may have lots of empty buildings, but it is still worth a visit. This town was once bustling from the copper mines nearby. In 1907, the Miami Land and Improvement Company bought a plot of land in the area known as Miami Flats, which is now where present-day downtown Miami is located. The company continued buying more property around the original parcel of terra firma until 1909, when the train came rolling through town. On October 4th of that same year, they started selling and renting the plots of land. By 1910, the populace was over 800 souls living in Miami. When the copper mines dried up and closed down, Miami and its surrounding towns were hit hard.

Today, the downtown area is slowly being renovated, and the town offers low-cost and affordable housing.

VISITOR INFORMATION

**Globe-Miami Regional
Chamber of Commerce**

Website: www.globemiamichamber.com

Address: 1360 North Broad Street,
Globe, AZ 85501

Phone: (928) 425-3395 or 1(800) 804-5623

Email: visitorinfo@globemiamichamber.com

Miami has many amenities, such as hotels, antique shops, other stores, parks, historic sites, and several restaurants. When I am in Miami, I will usually eat at one of the two downtown Mexican restaurants, which have incredibly scrumptious food. Both are located on the main drag of downtown.

Guayo's El Rey

Address: 716 Sullivan Street, Miami, AZ 85539

Phone: (928) 473-9960

Chalo's Casa Reynoso

Address: 722 Sullivan Street, Miami, AZ 85539

Phone: (928) 473-8220

Overview of Miami from the road behind the apartments, 2010.

THE RELINQUISHED TRAILER PARK

Trailer Park, Mobile, 2011.

Mobile, Arizona, may not be one of those towns you would think to urban explore within, but we have found interesting abandoned places surrounding the tiny desert settlement. One of these places is located about thirty-five miles southeast of Phoenix and hidden amongst the trees along State Route 238. It is a small plot of land with several abandoned trailers and a child's swing set. At least this is what I saw the first time when I visited the place in 2010. Also, we were not sure if this area was a dumping ground for unwanted trailers, or a place where families once lived.

A partial and other trailer on the land, Mobile, 2010.

A child's playset, trailer park, Mobile, 2010.

An old trailer found on the property, Mobile, 2010.

Note: Use caution— either private property and/ or a dump. There are many hazards around this location.

The first time I visited the trailer park was in August of 2010. I don't know what we were thinking exploring this place in the dead of summer in Arizona. Not only was it over 100 degrees, but snakes and scorpions were out running wild that time of year. We had plenty of water and watched carefully every step we took as we walked around the area, noticing the ground was littered with debris and broken furniture. There were three trailers standing along with a swing set and remnants of a hobo camp. Inside the largest trailer there were ravished furniture and other items tossed all over the

The last trailer standing, Mobile, 2012.

Slide from child's playset now lying on the ground, Mobile, 2012.

place. Another trailer was leaning a bit, while the third trailer was slowing crumbling down. Near this third trailer was the swing set and plastic slide sitting on a wood base. Lying by the swing was a stuffed bunny that perhaps a little boy or girl once played with. Beyond the trailers and hidden in the shabby trees were traces of items as if someone once may have lived there. The space was cluttered with garbage, old mattresses, and rotting food. We walked around and quickly took pictures of as much as we could before jumping back into the air-conditioned car.

When we went back two years later, the place looked entirely different. I am not sure if the Arizona heat messed up our logical thinking, but my friend and I went back in July of 2012 during another hot summer. The first thing we noticed when we approached the trailer park was one trailer standing by itself. This solitary trailer was just a shell of what it once was. There was still a disorganized mess inside. We observed the massive amount of debris on the ground leading us to speculate that the other trailers were destroyed instead of being moved. It looked as if a tornado went through the area and ate everything in sight except the one lone trailer. The slide was lying on the ground and appeared to be all that remained of the swing set. It was amazing to me how much the place changed in two years. Even though it was very hot and it looked like a bomb destroyed most of the site, I still found it an excellent place for urban exploration photography.

I did return to the place in March of 2013 and it looked about the same as it did the previous year. This time, I concentrated on taking photos of all the interesting things I found on site.

A view of the property, Mobile, 2012.

Be sure to take a moment to roam around Mobile. This minuscule town is about thirty-five miles southwest of Phoenix on State Route 238. The desolate settlement was where the first black community existed in Arizona.

In the 1920s, the railroad companies referred to a portion of land in Arizona as "Mobile," and by the 1930s, the town was founded with some of its residents being of African-American descent. Two railroad cars were used as schools and children were segregated by color: One car was for the white children and the other was for the African-American children. Many of the African-American pioneers living in Mobile established places of their own that were called, "Negro Flats." This place also had tanks where baptisms were performed. The tanks were basically cattle watering holes in the desert. Cowboys would stand by and poke fun at their beliefs during the many baptisms.

In the 1950s, Mobile experienced its highest population count of around 400 people. With this quantity of individuals living in the community, the town became deficient in places of employment, running water, and learning accommodations. Shortly afterwards, many of the people departed from the settlement, leaving it an essential ghost town.

Galilee Baptist Cemetery sign (created by Sharon Day), Miami, 2010.

Estrella Mountains, 2010.

The burned-down house and barn found near the cemetery, Miami, 2010.

VISITOR INFORMATION

Today, this tiny desert town has less than 100 people calling it home. As you cruise around, you will notice scattered houses, the abandoned trailer park, mounds of landfills, and the small Galilee Cemetery. The cemetery is located off highway 238 and near the Mobile elementary school.

Off in the distance are the Estrella Mountains where many UFO sightings have been reported. During the cooler times of the year, areas in Mobile are great locations to park your car, pull out the folding chairs, the cooler, and do some UFO watching.

THE SUGAR BEET FACTORY

On 52nd Avenue and Lamar Road in Glendale sits an enormous and empty red-brick factory. On August 11, 1906, the Sugar Beet Factory was constructed just a mile from Glendale's business district. It was at 1:30 p.m. when general manager Lafayette Meyers flicked the switch, setting in motion all the equipment. Many of the local populace was there for the historic event. Six days after the circuits were turned on, bags of sugar came off the line. The sugar was rich in color and high-grade quality. Sugar beets became a very popular source to turn into granulated sugar. Glendale was a prime location with all its canals and irrigation systems for a sugar beet factory to be built.

Sugar Beet Factory, 2010,
Glendale, Arizona

Southside of the main building, Sugar Beet Factory, Glendale, 2010.

The main building was five stories high in one area and three stories in the rest of the structure. It was surrounded by a boiler house, a lime kiln house, a repair shop, and a 165-foot smoke stack with a 30' x 30' base. Also on the land were a sugar warehouse, beet sheds, and an office building. After only one month in operation, the Eastern Sugar Company had to shut down. Several factors caused the closure, such as the muddy canal waters were making the sugar very dark resulting in a lower quality product than other states that were producing sugar. Another problem was the lack of experience amongst the workers. Most of them were hired right before the

Office building, Sugar Beet Factory, Glendale, 2010.

Main building, Sugar Beet Factory, Glendale, 2010.

factory was opened and they had no sugar beet assembly experience.

In December of 1906, owner W. J. Murphy announced the factory would not be active in 1907 because of lack of water used for the crops. Starting in 1908, and after many years of changes and owners, the Sugar Beet Factory shut its doors for good in 1985. In 1979, the Sugar Beet Factory was placed on the National Register of Historic Places.

Today, the building is just a shell of what it once was. There are plans to restore the five-story structure into a liquor manufacturer and distribution company. The main building will be where the liquor will be prepared and the smaller storage house will be the tasting room.

Downtown Glendale, 2011.

a state. Another newspaper followed a few years later, as well as a high school and other establishments.

Today, Glendale has gained fame from hosting famous sports events. The historic downtown has many antique shops, various businesses, and several restaurants worth checking out. With over 230,000 people living and working in this city, Glendale is deserving of your attention.

The Sugar Beet Factory's building sits in the middle of Glendale, Arizona. The city of Glendale was officially founded on February 27, 1892, after canals were built and people arrived to colonize the area. Three years later, a school was constructed, the Glendale Grammar School. After the school opened, many people moved into the area and Glendale began to flourish. The Santa Fe Railroad's station was located in Glendale and became the trail connecting Phoenix, Prescott, and northern Arizona. The railroad made it possible for the people to move their products to the north and to have no trouble acquiring supplies for construction.

In the early 1900s, additional families moved to Glendale to live. Afterwards, a bank opened; many other businesses were soon to follow. In 1912, the city's first newspaper, *Glendale News*, rolled out its first publication. That happened the day after Arizona became

VISITOR INFORMATION

Find out about Glendale's places to shop, dine, and stay. See what events are coming, find out about the sports, and read all about historic downtown Glendale.

City of Glendale

Websites: www.visitglendale.com and www.glendaleaz.com

Address: 5800 W. Glenn Drive, Suite 140, Glendale, AZ 85301

Phone: 1(877) 800-2601

Email: tourinfo@visitglendale.com

Cerreta Candy Company, Glendale, 2011.

In the downtown area sits the family-owned business, Cerreta Candy Company. The large red-brick building has been located in Glendale for over forty years and was founded by Jim Cerreta Sr. Jim learned his candy-making skills from his father-in-law's factory in Ohio. Now the entire Cerreta family is into the chocolate and candy-making business. The family provides a thirty-minute guided tour showing how the candy is made. At the end, visitors are treated to a freshly made piece of candy and can then purchase as many sweets as can be handled in their store.

VISITOR INFORMATION

Website: www.cerreta.com

Address: 5345 W. Glendale Avenue, Glendale, AZ 85301

Phone: (623) 930-1000

Tour: 10 a.m. to 1 p.m., Monday to Friday; if you are a group of thirty or more, call to set up a private tour.

Every year, on the weekend before Valentine's Day, Cerreta's sponsors an event known as The Chocolate Affaire. This sweet-lovers experience can be found in the center of Historic Downtown Glendale in Murphy Park.

Besides all the tasty treats, this phenomenon has all types of activities for people of all ages to be a part of. In the evening, you can enjoy the sounds of various types of musical entertainment in the grassy concert hall. For more information, call (623) 930-2299 or visit their website at www.glendaleaz.com/events.

SAHUARO RANCH PARK HISTORIC AREA

Sahuaro Ranch Park entrance sign, Glendale, 2011.

Another place to visit while in Glendale is the Sahuaro Ranch Park Historic Area. This momentous gem is located north of Glendale Community College on 59th Avenue. Sitting on seventeen acres, it is surrounded by tall trees and is the city's oldest and greatest exceptional ranch. The 1885 homestead consists of thirteen original buildings, a beautiful rose garden, a barnyard, and notable orchards on well-preserved land. The park is listed on the National Register of Historical Places and referred to as the "Showplace of the Valley."

The homestead was constructed by William Henry Bartlett in the late 1800s. It

Bartlett House, Sahuaro Ranch Park, Glendale, 2011.

started with a large two-story home for Bartlett and his family. He had several structures built on the land, such as homes for the ranch hands, friends, and other family members. Afterwards, he added the barn and blacksmith shop and then the most amazing garden. The garden consists of various colors of rose bushes, trees, plants, with a large pond and bridge that takes visitors to the gazebo on the island. Eventually, electricity was added to the ranch along with an electrical generator to pump water from a well. Bartlett lived on the ranch until his death in 1918.

After Bartlett's death, the ranch had several owners until 1977, when the City of Glendale acquired the ranch, making it an historical area. Visitors to the park can take a self-guided tour to the several structures on the land. Each has a marker in front explaining who may have lived there. Moreover, scattered around and near each building are old rusty farm equipment and tools, and chickens and roosters roam freely around the park. The springtime is the best time to visit and wander through the beautiful garden as all the flowers are in bloom. There is a sense of the grand history at the ranch and spirits of times past still seem to be living there as you walk around the grounds.

VISITOR INFORMATION

Website:
www.glendaleaz.com/srpha

Address: 9802 N. 59th Avenue, Glendale, AZ 85302

Phone: (623) 930-4200

Open: 6 a.m. to sunset

THE DOMES

The Domes, Casa Grande, 2011.

On the outskirts of southern Casa Grande, south of Interstate 8, and on Thornton Road, stands a place known as The Domes. As you drive up the dirt road and amongst the scattered homes, you will notice some odd-shaped structures. One shape looks like a UFO flying saucer and the others resemble giant caterpillars. When you approach the place, you feel like you have just entered *The Twilight Zone*. What was this place and why was it built in this desolate location?

In July of 1982, Patricia Zebb, owner of InnerConn Technology Inc., was speaking to a group of around seventy-five people about her new computer manufacturing company. Her plan was to move the company headquarters

Inside "saucer-like" dome, Casa Grande, 2011.

from California to the newly constructed site in Casa Grande she called, "The Domes." She'd picked an isolated section of town, and had the buildings constructed of Thermoshell materials. The dome shape would be cost-efficient and perfect insulation for the hot Arizona months. The Domes were constructed by pouring three inches of polyurethane and then three inches of concrete against a balloon, the inside of which was held up by a steel skeleton. Zebb was very excited about the new plant and couldn't wait for that first circuit board to roll off the assembly line. It took six weeks to build, but sadly it never saw one item completed. Right after the dedication in 1983, InnerConn defaulted on a loan and the bank took over ownership. The site was purchased in 2006, but remains empty to this day.

Back dome, Casa Grande, 2011.

Throughout the years, time has been cruel to The Domes. The difficult weather has played havoc on the structures' now-crumbling walls and ceilings. Huge chunks of the ceiling lay on the floor, especially in the furthest structure. All the walls display graffiti, and trash has been thrown everywhere. This was the location where the youth hung out with friends and had crazy parties.

Walking through each building, the place has an eerie echo. Even though it was over 100 degrees outside when we visited, it was much cooler inside The Domes. With the difficult

Inside back dome, Casa Grade, 2011.

127

weather and merciless sun of the Southwest desert, they are slowly disintegrating.

If you are into the paranormal and ghost hunting, The Domes would be the perfect place to visit. This spooky, odd-shaped place has rumors of ghosts wandering around each of the structures. People have reported hearing footsteps and whispering in the crumbling back Dome. A dark shadow-like shape has been reported wandering from structure to structure and the surrounding desert. Whatever the rumors are about The Domes, it is certainly an appealing place to check out. It is also an amazing place to urban explore and capture many pictures or videos of the unique buildings.

VISITOR INFORMATION

Contact the owner, Dan, for fees to visit or rent the Domes. It is a great place to do a ghost hunt.

Phone: (520) 423-0785

CASA GRANDE

Casa Grande has several places to visit for the tourist and urban explorer. The town originated in 1879, with the name Casa Grande meaning "large house" in Spanish. It started out as a community named Terminus, which meant "end-of-the-line." It kept that name until September 1880, when the railroad officials changed its name to Casa Grande after the Hohokam Ruins in close proximity to the settlement. The town was overcome by fires in 1886 and again in 1893, which wiped out every wood house and other buildings in the area. In the 1890s, when the mines dried up and finally shut down, Casa Grande almost became a ghost town. In 1915, the town was incorporated and remains quite vibrant to this day. The town survives now from its many retail trades, manufacturing companies, and agriculture.

Downtown historic Casa Grande, 2011.

While in town, don't forget to stop by the historic downtown of Casa Grande. The town has many restaurants and hotels for those visiting and weary travelers who need a place to lay their heads.

Besides The Domes, my friend and I found many other abandoned sites while driving around the area where urban explorers might enjoy photographing. The nearby Casa Grande Ruins are worth a visit. (To find out more about these ruins and where they are located, check out Chapter 1.)

VISITOR INFORMATION

City of Casa Grande

Website: www.casagrandeaz.gov/ web/guest/overview

Phone: (520) 421-8600

SUNSET COURT HOTEL

Sunset Court Hotel, Casa Grande, 2011.

On the main street, Interstate 8, we came across a deserted hotel, Sunset Court Hotel. The first time we laid our eyes on this place was in November of 2010, when it had a chain-link fence surrounding the entire perimeter. When we drove by it two years later, the fence was gone. We knew we had to stop and photograph this wonderful hotel with its small cabins dotting the front entrance. We parked near the pool in the back and began shooting tons of pictures. Not only were the pool, main building, and cabins interesting, but many other objects on the property, such as a boat, were thrilling to snap photos of as well. We even ventured inside and were able to get many more photos. The sun seeped through the many holes in the walls, ceiling, and doors to give us that perfect picture. It was an amazing place to urban explore.

Nine months later, we found ourselves in Casa Grande once again. We were there to revisit the many abandoned places we found on our earlier trips. When we drove past the Sunset Court Hotel, we noticed the fence was back around the entire perimeter except the pool. We wanted to take updated photos, so we stopped anyway. Even though we could not enter the property and go inside the main building, we still took pictures.

SLAUGHTERHOUSE

Every time we mentioned going to Casa Grande to friends, they told us that we must check out the place known as the "Slaughterhouse." We were able to get in contact with a Casa Grande resident who led us to the place in July of 2011. It was hot walking around the decaying house and barn, but well worth it. The house was missing its ceiling in the majority of the structure, except in one area. We were not able to go inside the covered space because there were many bees occupying the room. Graffiti covered many of the walls, even in the barn. The barn's roof was falling down and a mummified puppy was lying in the doorway of one of the tiny rooms. Although it was hot and a bit unsafe, we were able to take tons of pictures.

Whenever we return to Casa Grande, we always drive past the Slaughterhouse. The last time we went by, a squatter had made the place his home. He made a "No Trespassing" sign, hung a skull and cross bones flag, and had his dogs stare down anyone who dared to step on the property. The property is near Interstate 10 in Casa Grande.

"Slaughterhouse," Casa Grande, 2011.

The barn next to the "Slaughterhouse," Casa Grande, 2012.

HAYDEN FLOUR MILL

For more than fifteen years, the Hayden Flour Mill stood abandoned in Tempe, Arizona. With the help of volunteers and funds raised, the exterior of the mill has been restored. The chain-link fence that surrounded the place has been taken down for people to check out the grounds of this historic site. The interior of the mill is still going through renovations, but visitors can peak in the doors and windows to get a glimpse of the construction. Eventually, there will be shops, restaurants, and a place to watch

Hayden Flour Mill, Tempe, 2012.

movies, see a concert, and even to get married inside the walls of the old mill. With its location near Arizona State University and the Tempe's Town Lake, the Hayden Flour Mill will be the hotspot for locals and visitors alike.

In 1874, the first mill was an adobe building and held the sacks of flour on the second floor. It was well known around the Arizona Territory for hauling products in freight wagons and pack-trains to all the surrounding mining camps and military posts. It is estimated that over a million dollars worth of products went through the mill. The Salt River Pima Indians grew wheat, which was taken to the mill by horseback and traded for supplies. The mill became the main trade hub for all of the south side of the Salt River Valley.

Tempe was once a small town and surrounded by farmland as far as the eye can see. The economy was prospering because of the abundance of grain, cotton, fruit, vegetables, and dairy products found and grown in the area.

On July 10, 1918, after the old adobe building burnt down, a concrete mill was built in its place by J. C. Steele. The massive silos were the biggest undertaking for Steele, who constructed them of cast-in-place concrete posts, beams, and integral slabs. Most of the mills seeds came from grain grown in Central Arizona and it produced some well-known flours, such as Sifted Snow, Arizona Rose, and Family Kitchen to name a few. In 1951, the grain elevator and silos were built and located on the east side of the mill. Until 2007, they were the tallest structures in Tempe.

By October 10, 1984, the mill was added to the National Register of Historic Places. The Hayden Flour Mill stopped all operations on April 1, 1998, by Bay State Milling. At the time of closure, it was the most extended

Side of Hayden Flour Mill and silos, Tempe, 2012.

uninterrupted service for an industrial building in the valley. The mill and silos were left abandoned until fifteen years later when it was finally renovated.

I got the opportunity to visit this fantastic historic site and was thrilled at how rustic it still was. The grounds were full of flowers, bushes, trees, and a groomed grass lawn. We could not go inside the mill because it was locked up for renovation. However, we could see within the building where old, rusty machines and a huge safe still stood in locations where they were once in use. Today, this structure stands as the oldest cast-in-place, reinforced concrete building in Tempe. The building was constructed by procedures created after the massive San Francisco earthquake and fire of 1906.

Inside a machine room, Hayden Flour Mill, Tempe, 2012.

Hayden Flour Mill, Tempe, 2012.

VISITOR INFORMATION

Website: www.haydenflourmills.com

Address: 1195 S. Mill Avenue, Tempe, AZ 85281

Phone: (480) 355-6071

Directions: Located on Mill Avenue near Rio Salado Parkway in Tempe, Arizona.

TEMPE

Tempe Beach Park, Tempe, 2012.

The Hohokam first lived on the land now known as Tempe to build their canals. They left the area sometime in the 15th century, but some still remained. By the late 1800s, camps were set up along the Salt River to sell goods. These rustic shacks grew and eventually became settlements. One was named "Hayden's Ferry" after ferry operator, Charles T. Hayden, and the other was called "San Pablo." The river provided a quick transport for goods and building supplies.

In 1879, Hayden's Ferry was changed to Tempe and a school was built. This establishment was first called Territorial Normal School and is today known as Arizona State University.

The railroad was constructed in 1877, crossing the Salt River, linking Tempe to many other cities. Tempe officially became a city in 1894 and was the major central financial source for the entire rural region.

Today, Tempe offers many exciting tourist attractions. Mill Avenue, where the flour mill is located, has many quirky and notable shops, cafés, restaurants, and other businesses. Every spring it hosts the "Tempe Festival of the Arts." For information of the places to visit, events, hotels, eating establishments, Tempe Marketplace, Tempe Town Lake, and the historic sites of Tempe, Arizona, check out the following:

VISITOR INFORMATION

City of Tempe Tourism

Website:

www.tempe.gov and www.tempetourism.com/

Phone: 1 (866) 914-1052

Arizona State University

Website: www.asu.edu

Address: University Drive and Mill Avenue. Tempe, AZ

Phone: (480) 965-9011

ASU Gammage

Website: www.asugammage.com

Address: 1200 S. Forest Avenue, Tempe, AZ 85381

* On the campus of Arizona State University
Phone: (480) 965-3434 (Box Office)

Tempe Festival of the Arts

Website: www.tempefestivalofthearts.com

Address: 310 S. Mill Avenue, Tempe, AZ 85281

Phone: (602) 997-2581

Monti's La Casa Vieja (restaurant)

Website: www.montis.com

Address: 100 S. Mill Avenue, Tempe, AZ 85281

Phone: (480) 967-7594

CHAPTER 5

Languishing Cemeteries

Fairbank Cemetery, Fairbank, 2011.

If you love to explore spooky cemeteries, and take photos of remarkable headstones, this Chapter is for you. I have been to several of the old Wild West graveyards around the state of Arizona and I will take you to some of my favorite ones. Most of them are found in the middle of the desert near small mining towns. When these cemeteries were established, the surrounding shrubbery was green and flourishing. The land was dirt, but was kept well-groomed. Each headstone was picked out

with loving care with the name of the deceased person clearly etched on it. Some graves had obvious concrete or wood headstones, while others were marked with wood crosses or else nothing at all. Some people buried in these graves may be well known, but most are unfamiliar souls who once lived in Arizona during the Wild West era.

Decades later, most of these cemeteries are all but forgotten. Some are in terrible disarray, making it hard to recognize the location of each grave. Many years of the unsympathetic desert weather has rusted the metal fences, and rotted out the wooden ones. The climate and vandals have taken a toll on the headstones as well. Many are broken and crumbling, with the name of the deceased person barely visible. Some of the cemeteries are being maintained by various committees, but others are languishing and slowing dying in the Arizona desert.

ADAMSVILLE

It was in the 1870s when Charles Adams from Ohio purchased land in the Arizona Territory near the Gila River. He would name his place "Adamsville," with ideas of turning the dry piece of earth into a thriving farmland. He worked diligently removing shrubbery and digging ditches, so he could plant his grain. He saw his crops prosper and his dreams of turning Adamsville into a flourishing farming town. Shortly after the crops were growing well, a store and post office were built. By 1871, the overland mail stage stopped in town where, by this time, stores, homes, a flour mill, and water tanks now existed. The town hit its peak of 400 residents in 1872, growing in a short amount of time.

Water Towers, Adamsville, 2010.

Even Charles Adams, however, didn't realize that his dream of a town was sitting on the flood plains of Arizona. In 1900, the town and surrounding area experienced a severe rainstorm, causing the Gila River to rise and run over its banks. The water surged towards Adamsville

Adamsville Cemetery, 2010.

Adamsville Cemetery, 2010.

and completely wiped out the entire town. All the buildings and vegetation were utterly destroyed. Many of the residents were forced to flee to the nearby town of Florence two miles away.

Today, all that remains of Adamsville are the cemetery, old flour mill, some ruins, water tanks, and a sign that displays the town's name. Restoration of the cemetery was started in 1973 by Dr. Bertram Snyder and is well-maintained by the town. In 1992, a sign was erected at the entrance of the cemetery, but now all that remains are the posts. Surrounding the area is a rusty, worn-out, barbed-wire fence.

The cemetery is located at the south end of the town of Florence on the junction of Highway 79 and 287. The road curves to the right and the driveway is on the left to the entrance of the A.O.U.W. (Ancient Order of United Workmen) cemetery. Some of the earlier graves date as far back as 1877, but it is uncertain how many unmarked graves are there.

Adamsville Cemetery wheel symbol, 2010.

VISITOR INFORMATION

Pinal County Historical Society Museum

Website: www.pinalcountyhistoricalmuseum.org

Address: 715 S. Main Street, Florence, AZ 85232

Phone: (520) 868-4382

Email: pchsmuseum@yahoo.com

Downtown Historic Florence, 2010.

Ernest W. McFarland Museum, Library and Archives, Florence, 2010.

100 structures listed on the National Historic Registry. It has the largest Arizona State Prison complex, and an unspoiled Main Street where the movie *Murphy's Romance* was filmed. Just north of Florence sits the location of the largest prisoner of war camp called, "Camp Florence." The World War II site was built in 1942-43 and it held thousands of POWs on five acres. On the land were barracks, a hospital, a bakery, a swimming pool, athletic fields, and a few theatres. Today, the Florence Health Service Clinic sits in its place and serves the Immigration and Customs Enforcement (ICE).

Located in historic downtown Florence is the McFarland Museum and State Historic Park. The original courthouse is in the park and is in remarkable condition. The primary building was constructed in 1878, followed by the jail in 1882, and then the courthouse in 1891. The park and museum were named after Ernest McFarland, who once served as a U.S. Senator, Chief Justice of the Arizona Supreme Court, and the Governor of Arizona. He purchased the initial building in 1974, gave it to the state of Arizona, and then financed all the restoration to bring the building back to its original state. On October 10, 1979, the park was finally accessible to all who lived in and visited Florence.

After you visit Adamsville and its historic cemetery, take a short drive to the nearby town of Florence. With roughly 23,000 citizens living in town, this place is the oldest municipality in the country and has over

Silver King Market Place, Florence, 2010.

Back of Silver King Market Place, Florence, 2010.

In 1876, William Long was the person behind the construction of the Silver King Hotel in Florence. He was a colleague in the Silver King Mine that was located thirty-five miles from Globe. When the hotel was first built, it was an L-shaped adobe building, until 1893, when a fire destroyed the front of the hotel. Sometime in 1895, the hotel was renovated into the two-story red-brick building you see today.

VISITOR INFORMATION

The Silver King (Hotel) Market Place

Website: www.historic-hotels-lodges.com/arizona/silver-king-hotel/silver-king-hotel.htm

Address: Corner of Main and Sixth Streets, Florence, AZ

To find all the information, places of interests, eating establishments, shops, and hotels on the town of Florence, check out the following:

Town of Florence

Website: www.florenceaz.gov and http://visitflorenceaz.com

Address: 775 N. Main Street (P.O. Box 2670), Florence, AZ 85132

Phone: (520) 868-7500

OLD CONGRESS CEMETERY

Located northeast of Wickenburg on AZ Hwy 93 and then north on SR 89 is the diminutive town of Congress. It originated in 1884 after Dennis May revealed his finding of gold nuggets in the area. Congress was divided into two separate areas: Mill Town and Lower Town. Mill Town was located near the mines and where the company's offices, hospital, and residents could be found. Located in the southern part of Congress was Lower Town. In this area, the shops, restaurants, saloon, churches, and schools were placed along the main road. By 1887, the Congress Cemetery was developed nearby, and two years later, in January of 1889, the Congress post office was built. The town was

Old Congress Cemetery, Congress, Arizona, 2011

developing quickly, so, out of necessity, an electric light plant was constructed to handle all the needs of the people living there.

In 1893, the Santa Fe Railroad traveled through Congress Junction, which was located only three miles from the mine. Things changed for the mining town in the 1930s, when the mines shut their operations down. Once a thriving urban area that pumped out over 8 million dollars worth of gold, it then become a ghost town. The post office shut down and was moved to Congress Junction, where it remains to this day. Water became scarce, but because the railroad station remained active, some of the residents stayed.

Graves at the Old Congress Cemetery, Congress, 2011.

Today, all that remains of Lower Town are some old buildings and the Old Congress Cemetery. To get to the cemetery, take the dirt road off the main highway. In a couple of miles, you will see the gates of the old cemetery. The grounds are still maintained by the town's committee. As you look around, the place has that Old West, haunted look and feel to it. Most of the metal fences are rusty, and the wood fences are broken, as well as some of the headstones.

Not much is left of the town of Congress, which is located at the Old Congress Junction. There are a scattering of homes, businesses, restaurants, and hotels throughout this tiny mining ghost town. See the Visitor Information box on the next page for more information on the towns of Congress and nearby Wickenburg.

Graves at the Old Congress Cemetery, Congress, 2011.

Old wood headstone, Old Congress Cemetery, Congress, 2011.

Barely visible grave at the Old Congress Cemetery, Congress, 2011.

VISITOR INFORMATION

CONGRESS, AZ

www.city-data.com/city/Congress-Arizona.html
www.ghosttowns.com/states/az/congress.html

WICKENBURG

After you visit the Old Congress Cemetery, stop by the nearby city of Wickenburg. There you will enjoy the sites of the historic downtown area, quaint shops, and cafés. Stop by the Wickenburg Chamber of Commerce for all the information.

Wickenburg Chamber of Commerce

Website: www.WickenburgChamber.com

Address: 216 N. Frontier Street, Wickenburg, AZ 85390

Wickenburg Chamber of Congress, Wickenburg, 2012.

Phone: (928) 684-5479 or 1(800) 942-5242

Town of Wickenburg

www.ci.wickenburg.az.us

FAIRBANK CEMETERY

Wooden crosses, Fairbank Cemetery, 2011.

The Fairbank Cemetery is about one-half mile from the town and historic buildings of Fairbank Historic Town Site. The dirt trail is flat for most of the way, except when you get near the cemetery. The small dusty trail becomes steep along the side of a hill. On top of the hill are amazing views of the San Pedro River Valley, where the cemetery sits and only three graves are currently marked. Most of the graves were barely noticeable from the many years of abrasive weather and lightning strikes. Many of Fairbank's past residents are more than likely buried in those graves.

Fairbank Cemetery, Fairbank, 2011.

Graves, Fairbank Cemetery, 2011.

Grave, Fairbank Cemetery, 2011.

Antique teacher's desk, Fairbank Schoolhouse and Museum, Fairbank, 2011.

Inside Fairbank Schoolhouse and Museum, Fairbank, 2011.

VISITOR INFORMATION

San Pedro River Valley

www.sanpedroriver.org

Fairbank Historic Town Site
Directions: From Tucson, travel east on Interstate 10, then south on Highway 90 for about 18.5 miles to Highway 82. Turn left (east) and travel about 10 miles to the entrance on the left (north) side of the road (just east of the San Pedro River). The path to the cemetery is past the site where the structures and schoolhouse can be found. For the history of Fairbank, refer to Chapter 2, Fairbank (Historic Town Site).

GOODYEAR-OCOTILLO CEMETERY

Located in the heart of Chandler and hidden amongst Ocotillo's Fulton Ranch Community is the Goodyear-Ocotillo Cemetery. The 520-acre communal land was once known as Goodyear and built by the Goodyear Tire and Rubber Company in 1917. The place was made up of homes, cotton farms, hospitals, schools, chapels, a pool hall, and movie theaters. The cotton was processed to make the cords in the Goodyear tires. The community was started on a deal between Goodyear and A. J. Chandler. This transaction was for Chandler to rent 8,000 acres of land to house over 2,000 men who were hired

Cement grave with metal headstone, Goodyear-Ocotillo Cemetery, Chandler, 2011.

Goodyear-Ocotillo Cemetery, Chandler, 2011.

Metal headstone found at Goodyear-Ocotillo Cemetery, Chandler, 2011.

Metal and wood headstones, Goodyear-Ocotillo Cemetery, Chandler, 2011.

Broken cross and cement gave, Goodyear-Ocotillo Cemetery, Chandler, 2011.

to work at the ranch. They lived in small adobe houses or tents while using mules to move dirt and other rocks to clear the land for construction.

In 1943, Goodyear moved its operations to the West Valley, putting a halt to all the work done on the new community. After all that was said and done, the only things left of this once-thriving and hopeful community was 200 to 300 graves and a water tower. Most of the graves occupied were the remains of the workers at the Goodyear Ranch who had died between the years 1920 to 1962.

Today, the land is surrounded by a block wall in the middle of the prestigious community of Fulton Ranch, situated in the city of Chandler. It is located 0.1 mile south of Fulton Ranch Boulevard on South Iowa Street. The outside entrance is beautifully landscaped with flowers, bushes, grass, and a bench to rest on. The scenery inside the gates of the cemetery is quite unlike the outside. The grounds are dirt with tumbleweeds and no plant life anywhere, except for the tall dry grass. Scattered throughout are the grave markers and headstones. Many of them are broken and rusty from lack of care. The severe Arizona weather and vandals have raised havoc on this eerie little graveyard. The only signs of color

Park area outside the entrance of the Goodyear-Ocotillo Cemetery, Chandler, 2011.

Goodyear-Ocotillo Cemetery sign embedded in the wall, Chandler, 2011.

inside the walls are the few flowers put there by relatives or someone who cared.

Embedded in the wall and near the entrance of the cemetery is a plaque which reads:

This small plot of land was designated a cemetery by the Goodyear Tire and Rubber Company of Akron, Ohio. Goodyear owned and farmed the surrounding acreage from 1916 until 1943. Goodyear workers and their families are buried there. Local oral history indicated burials may have predated 1916. Preserved and signed by Fulton Homes, 2006.

VISITOR INFORMATION

City of Chandler, Arizona
www.chandleraz.gov

Chandler Office of Tourism
www.visitchandler.com

MORRISTOWN CEMETERY

Morristown Cemetery, Morristown, 2011.

Broken Morristown Cemetery sign, Morristown, 2012.

While driving northwest on Grand Avenue (AZ Hwy 60) from downtown Phoenix, there are several small towns and cities. One of these towns, located fifty miles up the highway, is the little community of Morristown. Within the town's perimeters is the Morristown Store, which was previously known as the Morristown Hotel. This building is on the National Register of Historical Places.

I have been to the Morristown Cemetery a couple of times. The cemetery is clean and looks as if some care is being thoughtfully taken of its appearance. At the entrance is a cracked, wood sign marking the cemetery's name. The first time I was there, the sign was intact, but with a crack running through the

Large bench found in Morristown Cemetery,
Morristown, 2011.

This image and two beneath:
Graves at Morristown Cemetery,
Morristown, 2011.

middle of the board. The second time I visited the cemetery, the bottom half of the sign was lying on the ground near the poles that held the rest of the sign. Also at the entrance is a pole with a tattered flag waving above. Some graves have noticeable headstones, while others have a large rock marking their sites. I did notice the fresh flowers adorning some of the graves. I felt the love and care from the families of those who have passed.

VISITOR INFORMATION

Directions: The Morristown Cemetery is located on Castle Hot Springs and Rockaway Roads, just off the junction of State route 74 and US Route 60 (Grand Avenue). Drive two blocks east of Highway 60 to find the entrance of the cemetery. Morristown is also located 11 miles south of Wickenburg, Arizona.

MAYER CEMETERY

Mayer Cemetery, Mayer, 2012.

Headless statue and cross dusted with snow, Mayer Cemetery, Mayer, April 2011.

Graves dusted with snow, Mayer Cemetery, Mayer, April 2011.

Mayer Cemetery covered with snow, Mayer, April 2011.

The first time I laid eyes on the Mayer Cemetery was in April of 2011. My friend and I were helping with a road game and the first stop for the participants was at the Mayer Cemetery. Arizona was experiencing an abnormal winter storm and it was snowing. By the time we got to the cemetery, it was covered with a blanket of snow. We stood inside the grounds waiting for the people taking part in the game to arrive. It was very cold and many of the headstones and shrubs had snow and icicles hanging from them. While we waited, we took many pictures of the graves and grounds blanketed in the stark white snow. It was a rare sight to see all that snow for a couple of ladies from Phoenix.

The second time I visited was in August of 2012. This time it was summer: the air was much hotter and there was no snow covering the land. I was able to get a better look at the grounds. The area was layered with overgrown weeds, cacti, and dried shrubbery. Some of the graves had broken crosses or statues and rusty metal fences. Even though the cemetery was unkempt, I still saw the beauty in the old burial place. This is definitely a great place to photograph for those who love to take pictures of a Wild West cemetery.

Mayer Cemetery, Mayer, 2012.

Graves at Mayer Cemetery, Mayer, 2012.

Headless statue and cross, Mayer Cemetery, Mayer, 2012.

VISITOR INFORMATION

Website: www.city-data.com/city/
Mayer-Arizona.html

Directions: AZ-69 to Pine Flats Road/
Forest 67 Road. Exit 262 toward
Prescott, left onto Central Avenue

Big Bug Station, Mayer, 2012.

The town of Mayer was named after its founder, Joseph Mayer, in 1881. Joseph traveled around Arizona mining in several places. Before landing in Mayer, he was living in a mining camp in the Bradshaw Mountains called, Tip Top. From there, he traveled to the banks of Big Bug Creek where he felt like he was home and put down roots. He purchased the Big Bug Station with gold and brought his family there to live. He had a home built along with a building for his business. This structure was constructed with porticoes in the front and back that extended from one end to the other. One side of the building was the general merchandise store with a bar and the other side was a restaurant.

Today, you can enjoy a great meal at the deli in the Big Bug Station. The bread is all freshly made daily. The cook is proud of his homemade horseradish sauce, which adds the right flavor to any sandwich. I shared pastrami on wheat with the horseradish sauce with my friend and it was the best I had ever eaten. I would recommend that if you find yourself in Mayer taking photos of the cemetery, be sure to stop at the Big Bug Station and give one of their sandwiches a try.

VISITOR INFORMATION

Big Bug Station

Website: www.bigbugstation.com

Hours: 6 a.m. to 3 p.m., 7 days a week

After enjoying a tasty breakfast or lunch at the Big Bug Station, walk next door to the adjoining Old Mayer Mercantile shop. The place is full of unique items and antiques. It is a wonderful place to spend time while visiting Mayer.

Old Mayer Mercantile

Website: www.merchantcircle.com

Address: 1278 Central Avenue, Mayer, AZ 86333

Phone: (928) 632-4177

CHAPTER 6

Mysterious Conundrums

Arizona desert, 2012.

For those who love the weird, mysterious, and paranormal, this chapter is for you. Arizona is a great big puzzle full of mystifying conundrums. Buried below the dusty desert floors, giant fossils of human and animal remains have been found. Along with the unusual bones and mummified humans, interesting creatures have been discovered in various places throughout the state. Seen wandering the barren desert are ghost camels with headless riders and other apparitions of people long since gone. Arizona is full of fascinating ghost stories of places hidden in the small mining towns or the big cities. Concealed in the mountains are treasures that have yet to be found and a castle made from various refurbished items. The mysterious perplexing wonders of the Arizona desert will always be a part of what makes this a wonderful place to live and visit.

In this chapter, I will provide you all the facts and the history of each place, person, or unusual conundrum. I will also take you to the location where each story was told and enlighten you with all the places to see while you are there.

MUMMIFIED BODIES

The Arizona desert might not be the first place you would think a mummified body would be found. However, on several occasions throughout history a carcass was discovered buried or lying on the desert floor in a dried-up condition.

SYLVESTER

One such mummy was that of a cowboy found near the town of Gila Bend. It was in 1895 when a couple of rough-riders traveling on their horses across the desert came across an unusual sight. It was a body of a man that appeared to have been lying on the desert floor for a brief period and looked well preserved. The cowboy mummy was given the name Sylvester and was thought to have once been a 19th century rancher or perhaps a gambler. Hypothetical stories started circulating about how Sylvester was probably caught cheating, then shot, and bled to death trying to escape. They go on to say that while fleeing, he fell off his horse, landed on the desert dirt, and was covered with blowing sands. The sands dried his body overnight, preserving the corpse and resulting in the mummified state he was found in.

Dust devil, Arizona desert, 2012.

Although that story might be a bit far-fetched, another more believable account was being told as well. The claims are he was found shortly after death and preserved in a high level of arsenic. Arsenic was used to stop the physical manifestation of a corpse rotting by killing bacteria and insects that invaded it. This custom of using arsenic was found to be poisonous by the 1900s and never used again. No one knows who preserved his body in arsenic, but his mummified figure was put on exhibit in a sideshow for all to see. The Wild West outlaw mummy was acquired by the Ye Olde Curiosity Shop in Seattle, Washington, in 1955, and put in a glass case for display. This has been Sylvester's home ever since.

VISITOR INFORMATION

Ye Olde Curiosity Shop

Website:
www.gilabendazchamber.com

Address: 1001 Alaskan Way (Pier 54), Seattle, WA 98104

Phone: (206) 682-5844

* More information on things to see while in Gila Bend can be found in Chapter 4, Discarded Motel.

THE THING

What is "The Thing"? Driving along Interstate 10 from Tucson to El Paso, Texas, you cannot help but notice bizarre billboards scattered along the route. The first one will simply say, "The Thing," followed by another a few miles later with the words, "What is it?" *Hmm*, your curiosity is now peaked as you drive by the next billboard with "Mystery of the Desert" advertised on the life-sized poster.

Located on a summit between Benson and Wilcox on exit 322 from Interstate 10, is a large red, yellow, and blue filling station and quirky little gift shop. Inside, you will find the typical Southwest roadside gifts, jewelry, Native American items, books, antiques, and, of course, "The Thing." There are even shirts, cups, shot glasses, and magnets advertising the mysterious conundrum. It is a clever promotional act to get people interested in visiting the shop so that they might see exactly what "The Thing" is.

A sign for "The Thing" along Interstate 10, 2012.

My curiosity about what "The Thing" really was, had my friend and I checking it out in February of 2014. We were told at the register that it would cost us one dollar to walk through a tiny courtyard and enter the museum. Located in the courtyard are three prefabricated, corrugated steel sheds full of odd exhibits. You will note the unusual wood carvings, framed lithographs, saddles, rifles, a covered wagon, and some vintage automobiles. One of the autos is a 1937 Rolls-Royce claimed to have been once owned by Adolf Hitler. After walking through a maze of bizarre stuff, visitors finally come upon the prize possession hidden in the back. "The Thing" is a mummified mother-and-child display encased in a glass-covered coffin. Is it real? Some will tell you it appears to be genuine, and some will say it is bogus. If this strange oddity peaks your interest and you want to see it for yourself, it will cost you a buck, but it's well worth the visit.

There isn't much information on how the mummies and their coffin ended up in the shop. The story is told that in 1965, a man named Thomas Brinkley Prince relocated his wacky retail business from California to Arizona, east of Benson. It is not clear how Prince acquired the extraordinary "Thing," but he publicly announced it as his main attraction for the shop. This advertisement is still found down Highway 10 on the mystifying billboards alongside the road.

VISITOR INFORMATION

The Thing?

Website: www.roadsideamerica.com/story/2023

Address: 2631 N. Johnson Road, Dragoon, Arizona

Phone: (520) 586-2581

Hours: 6:30 a.m. to dark (call to verify) daily

Directions: I-10 to exit 322, south side

Benson, Arizona

www.cityofbenson.com and www.bensonvisitorcenter.com

PREHISTORIC CLIFF DWELLER

Near the city of Prescott, in the mountains near the Verde River, a mummy of a prehistoric cliff dweller was discovered by John McCarty. He was recognized as an avid hunter and would often be found tracking in the northern section of Arizona. In March of 1896, he was hiking around cliffs near the Verde River, over ten miles north from the entrance of the East Verde. He tossed a piece of metal at the side of the rock cliffs and noticed that, when it made contact, it sounded as if there was an empty space in the wall. He examined the area and noticed an underground chamber with a mummified body inside. The body appeared to be sitting against the side of the cavity as if put there as a means of retribution. He was sealed in this tomb and probably met his demise by lack of food, water, or oxygen. McCarty found pottery shards, a stone axe, and arrowheads made from black glass and flint next to the torso. It looks as if this ancient man kept himself busy while serving out his punishment.

McCarty removed the twenty-one-pound mummy and placed it on bedding. A donkey pulled the body behind it through the dirt desert floors until arriving at the main road. From

Scenic overlook near Prescott, 2011.

there, it was taken to the nearby city of Prescott and examined. The mummy was a male and very well-preserved. Various locations on the body had holes where the bone was exposed. The bones looked like rawhide, but the skin was smooth. The mummy's head was a bit of puzzlement. The forehead receded from the nose, while the back of skull was large, a feature usually found in the early Aztec people. Skulls that were found in the Verde River location usually had a more Caucasian shape. The examiners could not explain why his cranium was shaped so oddly. He had a full set of teeth, which were in amazing condition. Any dentist would have been proud. As time went by, the mummy started crumbling a little at a time. To preserve it, McCarty coated it with varnish and placed it in a hermetically sealed glass-covered box.

I am not sure where the mummy can be found today. Some say he lies in his glass box somewhere in the city of Prescott.

If you are one who is fascinated by giant skeletons and bones, good news: some have

VISITOR INFORMATION

Prescott

www.cityofprescott.net and www.visit-prescott.com

* For more information on the City of Prescott, please refer to Chapter 3, Big Nose Kate.

GIANT SKELETONS, BONES, AND BIGFOOT

A GIANT IN CRITTENDEN

Jawbones found near "Slaughterhouse,"
Casa Grande, 2011.

been unearthed around Arizona. One such skeleton was discovered in 1891 near the town of Crittenden. While breaking ground for a commercial building, a giant stone coffin was uncovered. The project manager didn't want to open it until an expert was called in to examine the strange find. When it was finally opened, a granite case was found inside that appeared to have held a body of a man at least twelve feet tall. A carving on the casket pointed to the fact that he had six toes and fingers. In Biblical history they spoke of the giants during ancient times with six toes and fingers that roamed the world.

Crittenden was founded in the 1860s and was first recognized as Casa Blanca. The mines in the area were prosperous and a rail depot was constructed. In 1885, a two-story hotel was erected and, two years later, an earthquake marred the town's only established structure. Today, the hotel's second floor is missing, and those people who once lived there have gone, leaving Crittenden a ghost town.

Grand Canyon, 1995.

Another interesting story of skeletons and giant bones found in Arizona was at the Grand Canyon in 1923. While hiking around the canyon, Samuel Hubbard came across two petrified human remains. The skeletons measured around fifteen to eighteen feet in height. Each was rooted in the sandstone and formed of a limestone fossil. It took him days to dig out one of the skeletons because it was wedged under a rock fall. The other one was in a crevice and very tricky to access. He was able to take pictures of those remains.

The Grand Canyon is located in the northern part of Arizona and is a must-see place to visit. With approximately 5 million guests each year, this majestic place offers breathtaking views. Visitors can spend an entire day or two traveling around the park and get a different experience viewing the canyon from various locations. The canyon has several hotel choices, gift shops, the skywalk, picnic areas, and restaurants. Take a helicopter ride inside the canyon, hike down to the bottom, hire white-water raft trips on the Colorado River, or ride the rails from Williams, Arizona. If you are one who loves a paranormal experience, the Grand Canyon has had its fair share of ghost and UFO sightings, too.

Grand Canyon and Visitor Center, 1995.

VISITOR INFORMATION

Grand Canyon

Website: www.nps.gov/grca/index.htm

* The above site will help you to find all the information on the Grand Canyon you will need to make your visit a pleasant one.

Grand Canyon West and the Skywalk

Website: www.grandcanyonwest.com

Address: Grand Canyon Hualapai West entrance

Reservations:

1 (888) 868-9378 or 1 (928) 769-2636

Price: $25 per person (plus park entrance fees)

Directions: To find the west entrance to the canyon from Kingman, travel north on US 93, drive approximately 30 miles to the Pierce Ferry Road, and then turn right. Drive 28 miles to Diamond Bar Road; turn right; drive 14 miles on a dirt road and 7 more miles on a paved road to the Grand Canyon west entrance.

Grand Canyon Tours:

Website: www.canyontours.net

Phone: 1(800) 301-7152

Train near Visitor Center in Wickenburg, 2012.

In 1901, and when Arizona was just a territory, the Grand Canyon trains would take folks to the south rim of the canyon for a fun excursion. The train offered a nice, comfortable trip to the Grand Canyon for all men, women, and children. Some would choose to make it a day trip, while others decided to take a room at the lodge. These people stood at the rim and were taken in by the extraordinary beauty of the canyon, much like we do today.

In 1968, the trains quit traveling to the Grand Canyon when automobiles became trendy. People were opting to drive themselves to the park instead of spending the money on the train ride. In 1989, a group of businessmen purchased the Grand Canyon Railway, revamped the train, and found renewed interests from people wanting to take the historic ride. Today, many sit in comfort to take a fun day trip or several days' vacation using the Grand Canyon Railway as their mode of transportation.

VISITOR INFORMATION

A fun way to get to the Grand Canyon is to jump aboard the Grand Canyon Railway for a historic ride. This Polar Express-type experience offers four different packages, which start in Williams, AZ, and travels to the Grand Canyon National Park. Today, we can take the same route that generations before us traveled.

If you are interested in booking a ride you can go to their website, www.thetrain.com or call 1-800-THE-TRAIN.

The White Mountains, 2008.

Arizona might not be the place you would think the "big fella," also known as Bigfoot or Sasquatch, would be found, but sightings are reported all over the state. Surrounding the Sonoran desert are mountains with dense forests, abundant wildlife, serene lakes, and apparently Bigfoot. I have not witnessed one, but for those of you who are interested in possibly running into the big, hairy cryptic, I will list some of the hotspots where they have been spotted.

VISITOR INFORMATION

White Mountains
www.azwhitemountains.net

Mogollon Rim and Payson
www.paysonrimcountry.com

Coconino National Forest and Flagstaff
www.fs.usda.gov/coconino

Yavapai County and Prescott
www.yavapai.us

White Tanks
www.maricopa.gov/parks/white_tank

EXTRAORDINARY CASTLES

Scorpion Gulch, abandoned on South Mountain, Phoenix, 2011.

Arizona has its fair share of remarkable structures. Some of the buildings are businesses, while others are homes, either abandoned or still occupied. The historic buildings range from being constructed of wood, rocks, and even mud. The histories behind their facades are as interesting as their appearances. I will take you to a couple of the bygone castles of Arizona and give a brief history of each.

Tovrea Castle, Phoenix, 2011.

Tovrea Castle sits on the east side of Phoenix and is in the center of several acres. The castle is three stories and resembles a three-tiered wedding cake earning the name, "The Wedding Cake." Instead of being constructed with cake mixes and fondant, the castle's materials consist of wood and stucco in an ornate medieval fashion, imitating the styles from the home country of its builder.

In 1928, an Italian immigrant named Alessio Carraro purchased 277 acres of barren desert land and began the construction of Tovrea Castle. He had great visions of an extraordinary resort with a plush desert garden surrounding the locality and the castle as its centerpiece. With the vision of Russian gardener Moktachev, they began converting the desolate desert into an amazing desert garden. It took two years for the creation of the castle to be completed. Soon after construction was finished, Edward Tovrea, who owned land surrounding Carraro's, opened a meat-packing plant nearby. Not happy with Tovrea and other adjoining landowners bringing in livestock, Carraro sold the property, along with its remarkable structure, to Tovrea and his wife, Della, in 1931. In 1932, Edward Tovrea passed away and Della decided to keep the castle as her permanent home. After she married William Stuart, it became a winter home until after his death. She again lived at the residence full-time until her death in 1969. After her passing, the Tovrea family trust was in charge of the property, but neglected any maintenance that was needed, causing the place to simply diminish over time. The once-beautiful desert gardens were now dying and ignored with the cacti suffering the most damage. Also, the deserted castle was in poor shape, making the structure unlivable.

In 1993, the City of Phoenix obtained the land and its wedding cake building, deeming the place a historic structure. In 1990, Tovrea Castle and its surrounding land were listed as a historical property and, in 1996, added to the National Register of Historic Places.

Today, the castle has been going through restitution, while the gardens are being restored to their former glory. Tovrea Castle has been giving tours and opened its doors to the public in 2009. For those who love the paranormal, I hear the place is haunted.

Downtown Phoenix from South Mountain, 2011.

VISITOR INFORMATION

Website: www.tovreacastletours.com

Address: 5025 E. Van Buren, Phoenix, AZ 85008

Phone: (602) 256-3221

Castle Tours: January thru April – Fridays, Saturdays, and Sundays, 8:30 a.m. to 11:30 a.m.; May – Fridays, Saturdays, and Sundays, 7:30 a.m. to 10:30 a.m.; June and July – Fridays, Saturdays, and Sundays, 7:30 a.m.; August, closed; September – Fridays, Saturdays, and Sundays, 7:30 a.m.; October – Fridays, Saturdays, and Sundays, 7:30 a.m. to 10:30 a.m.; November and December – Fridays, Saturdays, and Sundays, 8:30 a.m. to 11:30 a.m. Hours are subject to change.

Fees: adults – $15; seniors (55+); military or students – $13; children (2 -12) – $10; children (Under 2) – free

* Due to occupancy limits, tours are limited to 14 people and therefore must be booked in advance at 1(800) 838-3006. Any "walk-in" tour requests will be based on availability only.

Directions: from north Phoenix, take the Loop 101 south to SR202 to the Red Mountain Freeway. At the Van Buren and 52nd Street exit (Exit 4), turn right; travel south on 52nd Street to Van Buren and turn right. Drive west on Van Buren a short distance to the entrance of Tovrea Castle, which will be on your left. From south, west, or east of Phoenix, take I-10 to SR202 to the Red Mountain Freeway. From there, the directions are the same.

Mystery Castle, South Mountain, 2011.

Mystery Castle is perched high on the north side of South Mountain with a spectacular view of downtown Phoenix from its locality. The dirt road leading to the castle's asphalt parking lot is located along the mountain roads inside the park. Approaching the structure, one can't help but notice the odd, attention-grabbing edifice. The building looks like a combination of a castle, fort, and cabin. In front is a long, wood balcony and towards the back are uniquely placed turrets and parapets. Wedged in the wall along the walkway leading to the entrance is a wagon wheel. There are strange items built into the exterior walls that don't seem to belong there. The entire castle is constructed from refurbished materials found in the area, such as river rock, railroad ties, discarded metals, copper, various types of glass, old car parts, boulders with petroglyphs, and furniture from abandoned buildings.

The person behind this unusual place is Boyce Luther Gulley, a family man who lived in Seattle, Washington, with his wife and daughter. He spent many years at the beach building sand castles with his little girl, Mary Lou. She was sad every time a tide would come in and wash away all their work. He promised that someday he would build her a huge castle she could live in and that wouldn't wash away by unforgiving water. In 1930, he was diagnosed with tuberculosis. After hearing the devastating news, he didn't want to burden his loved ones, so he headed south to Arizona. He never told them about the disease and disappeared without a trace.

Boyce did gradually feel better while constructing his castle on the side of South Mountain in the desert of Arizona. He built it of native stones and salvaged materials found in the surrounding area. It was approximately 8,000 square feet, has 18 rooms, 13 fireplaces, interesting parapets, and many small, recessed spaces. He furnished the place with Southwestern antiques and threw in some medieval items. It was in 1945 when he finally succumbed from his illness and died after finishing his castle.

It would be fifteen years before Mary Lou Gulley and her mother would find out what happened to their missing loved one. An Arizona lawyer sent them a notice that Boyce had passed away. Imagine their shock to find out that he had been living in Arizona this whole time, when they assumed he was dead. As soon as they found out about the castle, Mary Lou and her mother moved to Arizona. According to the will, they had to live in the castle three years, and then they were allowed to open a trapdoor, which had treasures hidden

Mystery Castle from the walkway, South Mountain, 2011.

Patio of Mystery Castle, South Mountain, 2011.

inside. Buried under the floorboards were two $500 bills, gold nuggets, and a Valentine's Day card Mary Lou made for her father when she was a little girl. She was touched by the card and that he saved it all those years. It wasn't long before she fell in love with her mystery castle. Her mother died in 1970 and Mary Lou lived in the house behind the castle. For many years she maintained the property, conducted tours, and loved telling her father's story. Some couples even got married in the wedding altar inside the main area until the mid-2000s when Mary Lou no longer allowed the ceremonies to be performed. On November 3, 2010, Mary Lou passed away. There are still tours conducted today and the property is kept preserved and maintained, looking the same as it did the day Boyce built it.

Chapel Room inside Mystery Castle, South Mountain, 2011.

Music Room inside Mystery Castle, South Mountain, 2011.

VISITOR INFORMATION

Website: www.discoverphoenixarizona. com/mystery-castle.html

Address: 800 E. Mineral Road, Phoenix, AZ 85042

Phone: (602) 268-1581

Hours: open from early October to end of May – Thursdays, Fridays, Saturdays, and Sundays; 11 a.m. to 4 p.m. (Be there before 3:30 p.m. to take the last tour.)

Fees: adults – $10; children (5-12) – $5; under 5 – free

* The fees are to maintain the property and they prefer cash.

THE SUPERSTITION MOUNTAINS

The Superstition Mountains, 2013.

There are lots of mysteries surrounding the Superstition Mountains, which are located thirty-five miles southeast of Phoenix. The range of mountains got their name from all the tragedies most of the gold seekers met while searching for the Lost Dutchman Gold Mine. The Native Americans believed the mountains to be cursed. They also believed the mountains are sacred and that if you remove minerals from the area, you will be cursed and die. Some of the lore spread throughout is regarding people who were decapitated looking for the Dutchman's treasure because of the dangerous

curse that plagues the mountains. One false move while hiking off the trails and you can be bitten by a rattlesnake or fall over 100 feet off the mountain. Things can go wrong on these mountains in a matter of minutes.

In July of 2010, three men decided to try their hand at finding the treasure. They headed out, armed with a treasure map that a Native American elder had given them. If they followed the map closely, it should have only taken them three days to find the treasure. What happened to them on the trails of the Superstition Mountains is a mystery, just like

The Superstition Mountains from Goldfield Ghost Town, 2013.

the place itself. Seven days after they started out on their journey, the search and rescue people were called. After several weeks of looking for the men in the grueling heat, the search was suspended.

In January of 2011, a man named Rick was hiking one of the trails. After walking a distance, he came across two bodies lying in the desert dirt. The bones were left in a disturbing manner as if they'd met with a violent death. Their bodies were identified as two of the three men who had set out looking for the gold in July of 2010. Two weeks later, the body of the third man was found and his bones were tossed all over the area where he was located. Many believe that the spirits killed them because of the curse. But the mountains were not finished punishing those involved with that particular treasure hunt. The Native American elder who provided them with the map died shortly after the bodies were found in a freak accident. He

fell into a bio-duct and his head was crushed. Was this the curse of the Lost Dutchman's Gold Mine?

Who is this Dutchman and why is his treasure's location such a mystery? His name was Jacob Waltz and he was actually a German miner. He was born in Germany in 1808 and later found himself in America. In 1845, he started his gold hunting in North Carolina and became a U. S. citizen in 1848, while living in Mississippi and following his dreams of striking it rich. After a few years of frustration, he decided to move to California, believing he would have better luck there. He got as far as the Bradshaw Mountains in Arizona and found enough gold with which to survive. By 1868, while in his fifties, he was able to purchase a 160-acre homestead near the Superstition Mountains where he did his mining. For over twenty years he mined the mountains and finally he found his treasure. Some believe he told his caretakers

Rusty miner's equipment, Superstition Mountains, 2013.

the whereabouts of the gold mine just before he died in 1891.

There were many stories swirling around about how Waltz found the treasure. Some say he stumbled upon it, some say he killed other miners to claim the vein, while others believed he was given a map to its location. The only thing for sure was a cryptic message written by Waltz before he died:

From my mine you can see the military trail, but from the military trail you cannot see my mine. The rays of the setting sun shine into the entrance of my mine. There is a trick in the trail to my mine. My mine is located in a north-trending canyon. There is a rock face on the trail to my mine.

Even though the mysterious Lost Dutchman Gold Mine is one reason people visit the Superstition Mountains, the area offers many more points of interest to see. The nearest city to the peaks is Apache Junction. This city has many accommodations if you have plans to visit the Superstition Mountains. The following information will point you to various restaurants, shops, and hotels located within the perimeters of the city.

"The Lost Dutchman" Jacob Waltz's headstone, Pioneer Cemetery, Phoenix, 2010.

VISITOR INFORMATION

Apache Junction

Website: www.ajcity.net

Apache Junction Chamber of Commerce

Website: www.AJChamber.com

Address: 567 W. Apache Trail, Apache Junction, AZ 85220

Phone: (480) 982-3141 or (480) 982-3234

SUPERSTITION MOUNTAIN MUSEUM

If you plan to visit these mysterious mountains, then you must first stop at the Superstition Mountain Museum. The building is located on the side of North Apache Trail as you drive towards the mountains from Apache Junction. Inside the main building is the museum and gift shop. Tour the museum to receive an interesting history of the mountains and the lore surrounding them. Outside the building, on the grounds, is a dirt path that takes you to the Elvis Memorial Chapel, Apacheland Barn, Twenty Stamp Mill, Gallows, and Windmill. Apacheland is where some movies were made and celebrities once walked.

Superstition Mountains Museum, 2013.

Website: www.superstitionmountainmuseum.org

Address: 4087 North Apache Trail, Apache Junction, AZ 85119

Phone: (480) 983-4888

GOLDFIELD GHOST TOWN AND MINE TOUR

Apacheland Barn, Superstition Mountains Museum, 2013.

Down the road from the museum is Goldfield Ghost Town and Mine Tour. Goldfield Ghost Town is "the valley's only authentic ghost town" and a great place to get that 1890s Old West experience. The Narrow Gauge Train takes you on a scenic ride around the town and through the desert. Tour the Goldfield Mine, pan for gold and keep what you find. This Wild West town has over twenty shops, exhibits, and attractions from the Old West. The saloon has tasty food and entertainment in the evenings.

Goldfield is located at the base of the Superstition Mountains, fifteen minutes from Mesa and forty minutes from Phoenix. It is open daily from 10 a.m. to 5 p.m.; (480) 983-0333; www.goldfieldghosttown.com.

Goldfield Ghost Town and Mine Tour, along the main street, 2013.

WEAVER'S NEEDLE

Tucked in the Superstition Mountains and named after Pauline Weaver, sits a 1,000 foot-rock column called Weaver's Needle. Seen for many miles, this boulder is made of "a thick layer of tuff (fused volcanic ash)," which was heavily eroded, resulting in an unusual peak with a split in the rock resembling the top of a needle. This split makes it look like it has two tops and is only visible on one side with many cacti surrounding it. Weaver's Needle is part of the legend of the Lost Dutchman's Gold Mine. It is said that the rock's shadow points to the area where the gold can be found. There are several trails that lead up to Freemont Saddle and offer an amazing view of Weaver's Needle. These trails are marked at the park's entrance near the parking lot off North Apache Trail.

Inside the Superstition Mountain Park, 2013.

CANYON LAKE

Another gorgeous place to visit surrounded by the Superstition Mountains is Canyon Lake. A few miles from Goldfield and around the winding roads lay a scenic body of water. The Canyon Lake area offers a camping ground, boat rentals, lakeside restaurant, and cantina, along with a cruise on a steamboat.

Canyon Lake Marina and Campground

Website: www.canyonlakemarina.com

Address: 16802 N.E. Highway 88, Tortilla Flat, AZ 85219-9898

Phone: (480) 288-9233

Canyon Lake sign, Superstition Mountains, 2013.

Canyon Lake, Superstition Mountains, 2013.

TORTILLA FLAT

Only a few miles from Canyon Lake, along the historic Apache Trail, and tucked inside the mountain's rocky ridge is traces of the Wild West town of Tortilla Flat. In 1904, the settlement served as a resting place for the stagecoach and its passengers. The town suffered fires and floods, but still endured.

When visiting Tortilla Flat, be sure to bring your appetite and have a meal at the Superstition Saloon and Restaurant. If you are not hungry, have a sit on the saddle bar stools at the saloon and kick back a cold one. The place is decorated with Old West flare and adorned with dollar bills from guests all over the world. If the meal doesn't fill you up, then stroll on down the road to the Country Store for dessert: they have tasty Prickly Pear ice cream. Their gift shop has all types of Native American items, clothes, and many more bizarre objects.

Tortilla Flat, with its population of 6, is another place inside the Superstition Mountain worth a stopover.

Website: www.tortillaflataz.com

Address: 20909 East Apache Trail, Tortilla Flat, AZ 85119

Phone: (480) 984-1776

Summer hours: June 1 to September 31 – 9 a.m. to 5 p.m. (Monday to Friday); 8 a.m. to 7 p.m. (Saturday and Sunday)

Winter hours: October 1 to May 31 – 9 a.m. to 6 p.m. (Monday to Friday); 8 a.m. to 7 p.m. (Saturday and Sunday)

MINING CAMP RESTAURANT AND TRADING POST

Consume a wonderful Old West meal at the Mining Camp Restaurant. In 1961, the Mining Camp Restaurant and Trading Post opened its doors to the public. The building was constructed of large Ponderosa Pine trees found in Payson. Today, it has a mining camp look and feel to it.

Mining Camp Restaurant, Superstition Mountains 2013.

Visitors first see a waiting area and then the trading post. From there, diners are seated at a picnic-like table with tin mine-camp plates, silverware, and cups provided. The waitress brings freshly baked rolls, baked beans, and coleslaw. We ordered the three-meat platter along with our beers. The two very hot platters had ribs, chicken, ham, stuffing, and baked potatoes. The entire meal was so delicious. After the meal, we were treated to the country western sounds of the McNasty Brothers. This is the perfect place to get that western BBQ cuisine.

Website: www.miningcamprestaurant.com

Address: 6100 East Mining Camp Street, Apache Junction, AZ 85119 (Located 4 miles east of Apache Junction on Highway 88)

Phone: (480) 982-3181

Table settings inside the Mining Camp Restaurant, Superstition Mountains, 2013.

UFOS

There is one other thing the Superstition Mountains are known for and that is all the UFO sightings. The Native Americans believe the little people or "Tuar-Tums" hide inside the rock walls of the mountains. They are sometimes spotted lurking on the rims, as if they are keeping watch over everyone who dare come near the mountains and its many caves.

Old West wagon with the Superstition Mountains at dusk, 2013.

There have been hundreds of reported claims of unusual lights in the skies over the mountains. Some are small and dim, while others are large and bright. Most are seen hovering and then quickly zipping away. Many UFO observers will park at one of the many picnic areas to see if they are lucky enough to catch a glimpse of a flying saucer.

VISITOR INFORMATION

If you are interested in booking a site for an overnight camping experience:

Lost Dutchman State Park

Website: http://azstateparks.com/Parks/LODU

Phone: (520) 586-2283 (Reservation Center)

Price: $5 non-refundable reservation fee per site.

* Reserve a campground, RV, or tent site.

CHAPTER 7

Strange Creatures

Gila Monster, Painted Rock, 2013.

Driving around the state, travelers will notice the many changes of scenery. There is the desert with its ample cacti and, a mile or two down the highway, the cacti seem to disappear. The further north and east you drive in the state, you will come upon a thick forest. The lakes in those areas may be abundant with water, while the desert lakes and rivers are dried up.

Along with the many different types of foliage adoring the scenery, there are critters and creatures as well. Typically, snakes, scorpions, and lizards can be seen roaming the dry desert floor, while larger animals have been seen in the forests. Once in a while, a rare creature, or its remains, has been discovered in the state.

MERMAID AND BLOWFISH

In the Wild West town of Tombstone, a couple of bizarre creatures lie in a display case at the Bird Cage Theatre. Upon first walking through the back door of the Bird Cage's museum, a glass box can be seen sitting on a shelf. Inside the box is a mummified small creature that resembles a mermaid. The bottom half looks like a fish with scales and fins, but the top half has the body of a human and a face like a monkey. In the upper portion of the glass box is a blowfish. It looks well-preserved with its mouth open and body all puffed out. How did two water creatures end up in a desert mining town?

What I was told about these strange little beings was that sometime in 1934, a mysterious person donated them to the Bird Cage Theatre's museum. It was rumored to have been a local businessman, Quong Lee, who once displayed the mermaid in his CanCan Café. He wanted to display it where all could see it, so he donated it to what he thought was Tombstone's museum. However, they came to be in the Bird Cage Theatre. You should make a point to see these water creatures and all the other original artifacts in the museum.

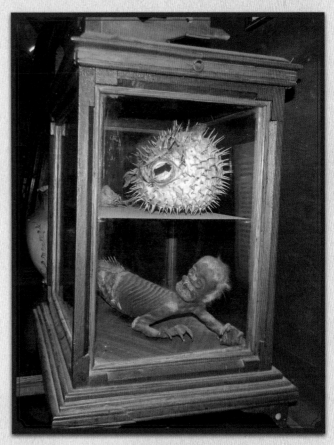

Bird Cage Theatre, Tombstone, 2011.

VISITOR INFORMATION

Bird Cage Theatre Museum

Website:
www.tombstonebirdcage.com

Address: 535 East Allan Street, Tombstone, AZ 85638

Phone: (520) 457-3421

Hours: 9 a.m. to 6 p.m.

Bird Cage Theatre, Tombstone, 2011.

THUNDERBIRD

The photo of a group of men standing around an enormous bird has been circulating around for many years. The photo's title is "Thunderbird" and it was told that the creature was captured near Tombstone, Arizona. Many question the authenticity of the photo and if the story was simply an urban legend. Whether it is true or not, the photo and story make for some interesting conversation.

This is the story I found while researching the picture: While walking in the Arizona desert in April of 1890, a couple of cowboys spotted a massive flying bird in the sky. The winged creature had a body around 92 feet long and was smooth like a serpent. The wingspan was about 160 feet with no feathers and resembled colossal bat wings. Its face looked like an alligator and it had two clawed

"Thunderbird." Unknown origin.

feet. The two men followed it on horseback, until their rides were too afraid to continue, and then they chased it on foot. They finally caught up with it and riddled the beast with bullets until it finally died. They snipped off a piece of its wing and brought it to Tombstone. The story of the two men and the huge bird was allegedly written in the Tombstone newspaper, the *Epitaph*, but employees of the paper searched the archives and found no such story or picture. Many questions are still swirling around about the story and the photo. If there were only two men who shot and killed the flying cryptic, then why are there six men in the photo? And what happened to the story written about their encounter?

VISITOR INFORMATION

Tombstone Epitaph
www.tombstoneepitaph.com

CHUPACABRA

There are many stories of dog-like creatures roaming around Arizona known as "Chupacabra" (goat sucker). Feared by many, these beasts have been rumored to tear apart livestock and consume their blood. One of the first reported sightings was in Tucson. Two men were roused out of bed by the loud shrieking of their goats. When they went to check to see what all the commotion was about, they saw a weird-looking beast on top of one of the goats. This dog-like creature looked at them, unleashed an eerie screech, and then scampered off.

In 2003, another sighting was reported that was similar to the first one. This was also in Tucson and the creature was seen cowering like a frog. It turned, jeered at the viewer, and then ran into the darkness.

Many believe the Chupacabra are real, while others feel they are just superstition made up to scare people. Real or not, there have been many sightings all over the southern part of Arizona.

Chupacabra, 2012.

GOMPHOTHERE

The bones of another very strange creature found in Arizona are that of a Gomphothere. What is that you ask? I wanted to know as well, so here is what I found: A Gomphothere is a faint kin to elephants with broad snouts and elongated jaws, similar to a crocodile. They were found in North America over 1 to 2 million years ago and were around nine feet tall with two or four tusks. The bones of these ancient animals have been found in the southern portion of Arizona near the Mexico border. They are believed to have vanished around the time humans started roaming the Earth.

ALLIGATOR-SNAPPING TURTLE

During a cleanup of the Phoenix Zoo pond in May of 2010, a sixty-two-pound "alligator-snapping turtle" was discovered. This creature has been described as "straight out of prehistoric times" and was found living in the deepest part of the pond located in front of the zoo. The jaws on this amphibian are strong and able to snap off a child's arm or leg. The Phoenix Herpetological Society says that this particular creature does not belong in Arizona. They believe it was an exotic pet belonging to someone who dumped it in the pond because they didn't want to take care of it anymore. They have no idea how long it was living there, but felt it survived on the ducks, fish, and other turtles that existed in and around the pond. Even though the snapping turtle has now been removed, the Phoenix Zoo is a great place to visit and spend the day watching all the wonderful animals.

VISITOR INFORMATION

Phoenix Zoo

Website: www.phoenixzoo.org

Address: 455 N. Galvin Parkway, Phoenix, AZ 85008

Phone: (602) 273-1341

Hours: 9 a.m. to 5 p.m. (January 7 to May); 7 a.m. to 2 p.m. (June to August); 9 a.m. to 5 p.m. (September to October); 9 a.m. to 5 p.m. (November to January 6)

Fees: adults – $20; seniors (60+) $15; children (3 to 12) $10; children (2 and under) free ; Phoenix Zoo member – free

* Early entry – Phoenix Zoo members may enter one hour early

WILDLIFE WORLD ZOO AND AQUARIUM

Sitting on 95 acres in Litchfield Park is the Wildlife World Zoo and Aquarium. It opened in 2008 and features African and South American animals. The aquarium holds a total of 180,000 gallons of water with thousands of different aquatic creatures. It is the permanent home to massive groups of unruly and endangered animals, birds, and sea creatures. You can take a train ride throughout the park to see many of the creatures in their own habitat. On January 25, 2014, a fifteen-acre Safari Park was added to the zoo with more places to eat, shaded viewing locations, new species of animals, and much more. You can walk the new addition or take the optional tram ride (for an extra fee). The Safari Park is included with general admission.

Entrance to the Wildlife World Zoo and Aquarium, Surprise, 2011.

Website: www.wildlifeworld.com

Address: 16501 W. Northern Avenue, Litchfield Park, AZ 85340

Phone: (623) 935-9453

Hours: 9 a.m. to 6 p.m. (last admission is at 5 p.m.); Aquarium exhibits – 9 a.m. to 9 p.m.; open seven day a week, 365 days a year, including all holidays

Prices: For Zoo and Aquarium; adults - $29 + tax; children (3 to 12) $14.25 + tax, children (under 3) free

* For special evening admission to Aquarium only (after 5 p.m.); adults - $16.99 + tax, children (3 to 12) $8.99 + tax, children (under 3) free

CHAPTER 8

Highway Ghosts

Arizona highway, 2011.

Arizona has many highways taking visitors all over the state. These roads travel though the desert, mountains, and take explorers to historic sites. The incredible scenery is not the only thing people have seen on their day or nighttime travels on the roads. Some have witnessed paranormal phenomena that they cannot explain. Claims have been made of ghostly animals, people, and objects as they have driven through the desert or hitched a ride. The next time you are on Arizona's highways, keep a sharp eye out for something, or someone, who may be spending eternity wandering Arizona.

GHOST CAMELS

Arizona desert, 2011.

People have seen ghost camels meandering the desert for decades. In 1857, camels were brought to the desert to move supplies across the Southwest for the army. Because camels required less water than horses and mules, could travel great distances without getting exhausted, and carry heavier loads, the War Department requisitioned the use of around seventy-two camels. It wasn't long before the camels' nasty dispositions and constant running off at night became a nuisance to the soldiers. After the Civil War, the camels were either auctioned off or simply let loose in the desert. The last of the camels found in the desert was in the early 1900s. It was captured and lived out its life at a zoo in California. Now all people get glimpses of are ghost camels that are still lost and roaming the desert.

One story is that of the "Red Ghost" camel and its headless rider. They say the rider was a young soldier who was deathly afraid of the camels. In order to help him get over his fear, they tied him on top of one and smacked the beast on its ass. The frightened animal ran off into the dark desert with its helpless rider, never to be seen again. Is he the headless rider people have reported seeing? If so, how did the poor man's head get severed from his body? I have no answers, but keep a lookout for both of them while traveling on the highways.

PHANTOM HITCHHIKER

Arizona highways seem to go on forever in some parts of the state. It is hard to not let your mind wander while traveling to a destination. Along the way you might run into a hitchhiker or two. Most of them are real-live people needing help getting to their journey's end, but there is one near the community of Anthem North that appears to be a phantom hitchhiker.

Anthem is located north of Phoenix on Black Canyon Highway (Interstate 17). A shadowy male figure has been seen along the highway holding a lantern. The Anthem Hitchhiker is the name he was given because of the location people have seen this ghostly figure. He appears to be waiting for someone to give him a ride, but there is one big problem: he is a ghost and has been dead for years.

Hitchhiker, 2012.

The story told of this unlucky gentleman was that he was hitchhiking and hit by a car on the very spot he is now seen. He was on his way to Phoenix, but never made it. Now he can be observed on the side of the road with his lantern trying to get a ride. Those who have dared to offer him a ride have pulled their vehicles over, only to witness him evaporate into thin air. Others who were not so brave would quickly drive by and look in their rear-view mirrors only to see him disappear before their eyes.

If you are ever traveling on Interstate 17 near Anthem when the skies are dark and the moon is out, beware of the phantom hitchhiker.

THE GHOST BUS OF UNION PASS

School bus, Miami, 2010.

If an eerie ghost camel or hitchhiker doesn't stir up your paranormal juices, how about a ghost bus? The Ghost Bus of Union Pass has been seen by many who travel on U.S. Highway 93 from Phoenix to Laughlin, Nevada. It was in July of the early 1990s when Bus 777 with its 48 passengers headed off from Phoenix to Laughlin. They were excited to relax and do some gambling at the casinos. The driver took U.S. Highway 93 and headed north to his destination. After a brief stop in Wickenburg, they continued on, but had bus problems along the way. The vehicle overheated when they stopped in Wikieup and the driver wanted to wait for another bus. The passengers were eager to start gambling and encouraged the driver to push on. By the time they got to Union Pass, the bus broke down again. The 48 passengers pushed the bus up the hill, quickly got in, and rode the bus down the other side. One witness said the bus was flying at a hasty pace and disappeared behind a hill. Bus 777, its driver, and passengers were never heard from again. The police were puzzled at the scene of the accident because they found no skid marks or any indication that a disaster of any kind had occurred at that location.

Three years after Bus 777 disappeared, people driving along Highway 93 began seeing a phantom bus near Union Pass. Usually, the witnesses were on the highway at night, traveling between Wickenburg and Wikieup, and noticed headlights rapidly approaching their vehicles. The driver would honk and was afraid of being hit by the oncoming bus.

To their shock and surprise, the bus lapses *through* their automobile, causing the driver and their passengers to scratch their heads in wonderment. Perhaps while you are traveling on Highway 93 near Union Pass, you might come across the ghost bus, too.

VISITOR INFORMATION

Wickenburg
www.ci.wickenburg.az.us

Laughlin, Nevada
www.visitlaughlin.com

DEVIL'S HIGHWAY

Objects, people, and animals are not the only things paranormal on the Arizona highways. How about a haunted highway for you to drive on? On the eastern border of Arizona, near Safford and Holbrook and up to the Four Corners, is Route 666, known as the Devil's Highway. Many bizarre stories have been told of people traveling on that highway. The road with its steep curves and dangerous switchbacks also has claims of ghosts, peculiar creatures, and UFOs scaring those who drive its eerie pavement. Other oddities reported are green lights accompanied by loud shrieking and a thick fog that surrounds vehicles.

In 2003, the Devil's Highway was renamed U.S. Route 491. Are people still experiencing weird phenomena on this highway after the name change? Why don't you travel on it and see for yourself.

Highway 491 (666) Sign, 2014.

Conclusion

I hope this trek to places around Arizona has gotten you excited enough to visit this diverse state! Arizona has lots to offer, so you will have plenty to do! Have a wonderful trip and be sure to take lots of photos!

Internet Sites and Visitor Resources

City of Globe; The Chamber of Commerce
www.globeaz.gov
www.gilacountyaz.gov
www.noftsgerhillinn.com
www.globemiamichamber.com; visitorinfo@
globemiamichamber.com

**National Monuments – Arizona; National
Park Service – U.S. Department of the
Interior**
www.nps.gov/moca

Tuzigoot National Monument
www.nps.gov/tuzi

Tonto National Forest
www.fs.usda.gov/tonto

Sierra Ancha Wilderness
www.wilderness.net
www.fs.fed.us

Gila Pueblo Project
www.statemuseum.arizona.edu/research/final_
sierra_ancha_rpt.shtml

**Casa Grande Ruins National Monument
Arizona**
www.nps.gov/cagr

National Park Service
www.nps.gov/petr
www.petroglyphs.us

**Sedona and Red Rock District Coconino
National Forest**
www.redrockcountry.org
www.visitsedona.com
Center for the New Age: http://
sedonanewagestore.com
Sedona Hiking: http://bestsedonahiking.com;
www.greatsedonahikes.com
Jeep Tours: http://pinkjeeptours.com/sedona/

our-tours; www.sedonajeeptours.com;
www.adayinthewest.com
UFO Tours: www.sedonaufoskytours.com
Tlaquepaque Arts and Crafts Village:
www.tlaq.com
Uptown Sedona: www.sedonacentralreservations.
com/shop-uptown-sedona.aspx
Coffee Pot Restaurant: www.coffeepotsedona.com
Red Planet Diner: www.redplanetdiner.net

Friends of the San Pedro River
www.sanpedroriver.org

The Fairbank Schoolhouse
Fairbank Historic Townsite:
schoolhouse@sanpedroriver.org
www.arizonaghosttowntrails.com/fairbank.html

Greater Bisbee Chamber of Commerce
www.bisbeearizona.com
www.discoverbisbee.com
www.cityofbisbee.com

Jerome Chamber of Commerce
www.jeromechamber.com
www.azjerome.com

City of Tombstone
www.tombstoneweb.com
www.cityoftombstone.com

Vulture Mine
www.travelchannel.com/tv-shows/ghost-
adventures
www.jpc-training.com/vulture.htm
www.desertusa.com
www.wickenburgchamber.com

The Clantons
www.clantongang.com/oldwest/famhist.html
www.bothillgraves.com
www.tombstonechamber.com/Boothill-
Graveyard

Springerville
www.springervilleaz.gov
www.arizonagravestones.org
www.findagrave.com
www.azhistcemeteries.org
www.legendsofamerica.com

Big Nose Kate
www.bignosekates.info
www.texasescapes.com
www.arizona-leisure.com/bird-cage-theatre.com
www.tombstonebirdcage.com

Gila Bend Chamber of Commerce
www.gilabendazchamber.com
www.gilabendaz.org

Glendale
www.azcentral.com
www.glendaleaz.com
www.molokane.org

The Domes
www.strangeusa.com
www.weirdus.com/states/arizona/abandoned/
domes/index.php

Hayden Flour Mill
www.tempe.gov
www.millavenue.com/go/hayden-flour-mill

Mayer
www.accessgenealogy.com/cemetery/arizona/
yavapai_county.htm
www.arizona.hometown.locator.com
www.city-data.com/city/Mayer-Arizona.html
www.city-data.com/city/Mayer-Arizona.html
Big Bug Station: www.bigbugstation.com
Old Mayer Mercantile: www.merchantcircle.com

Adamsville
www.ghosttowns.com/states/az/adamsville.
html

Congress
www.ghosttowns.com/states/az/congress.html
www.phoenixarizonarealestateblog.com/
goodyear-ocotillo-cemetery

Mummies
www.yeoldecuriosityshop.com/page/
mummyStory.html
www.seattletimes.com

Ghosts
www.legendsofamerica.com/we-ghostcamels.
html
www.examiner.com/article/red-ghost-and-hi-
jolly-of-quartzsite-az

www.outletsanthem.com
www.ci.wickenburg.az.us
www.visitlaughlin.com

Giants
www.ancientmoons.com/giants.htm
www.chapmanresearch.com
www.unexplained-mysteries.com
www.grandcanyonwest.com
www.canyontours.net
www.thetrain.com
White Mountains: www.azwhitemountains.net
Mogollon Rim and Payson:
www.paysonrimcountry.com
Coconino National Forest and Flagstaff:
www.fs.usda.gov/coconino
Yavapai County and Prescott: www.yavapai.us
White Tanks: www.maricopa.gov/parks/white_
tank

Superstition Mountains
www.prairieghosts.com/dutchman.html
www.ajpl.org (Apache Junction Public Library)
www.azstateparks.com/Parks/LODU/index.
html
www.ajcity.net
www.AJChamber.com
www.superstitionmountainmuseum.org
www.goldfieldghosttown.com.
www.canyonlakemarina.com
www.tortillaflataz.com
www.miningcamprestaurant.com
azstateparks.com/Parks/LODU

Castles
https://plus.google.com
www.phoenix.about.com
www.rvtravelog.com/mcastle.dir/mcastlel.htm
Tovrea Castle: www.tovreacastletours.com

Creatures
www.roadsideamerica.com/story/11288
www.tombstonebirdcage.com
www.cityofprescott.net
www.visit-prescott.com
www.phoenixzoo.org
www.wildlifeworld.com